MW01620266

DINO PEDRIALI

DINO PEDRIALI

Edited by Peter Weiermair

Texts by Maurizio Marini and Peter Weiermair

EDITION STEMMLE

Contents

"This new one answered to the more than ordinary name of Gianni; and he was as ordinary as his name. And it was this very ordinariness that made him so unbelievably beautiful. Viewed objectively, in fact, he was the most beautiful of them all. And above all he was the biggest by far; he also had the long, powerful legs of a football player, or of an athlete, at least. His hair was cut short: a thick, black down, though a few patches stood out like bristles on the forehead and the back of his neck. His face was so darkly tanned that this Gianni looked almost black: his tan was a little yellowish, like that of a Brazilian. And it hardly needs to be said that his eyes were large and black, gigantic and luminous like two moths; the nose was straight and narrow; the mouth was quite broad, and it shone just like the eyes. If you observed him more closely, though, his head looked a bit like the close-shorn melon of a new recruit (close-shorn, that is, in a somewhat demeaning manner, as is done with a boarding-school pupil or a man from a prison road-gang). But if he was [...] close-shorn because of sports, then that somehow gave him a kind of bourgeois touch."

"Gustarello's head was a true masterpiece of nature. His blond hair was golden, a kind of light polished gold. There were a few dark patches near the hairline, but everything above had a blinding lightness. He, too, wore a part on one side, but his hair was considerably longer and thicker than the curly-headed boy's, and the two crops of hair separated by the part looked like sheaves of wheat tangled by the wind under the rays of evening sun. His head was long, and so these capriciously curled masses of hair fell from his low forehead onto the back of his slim, bulging neck – like south Italians, especially Sicilians, often have – bringing out the full effect of his radiant beauty."

Pier Paolo Pasolini, "Petrolio", Berlin, 1994

Dino Pedriali's Work

Peter Weiermair

Dino Pedriali's work represents an extaordinary achievement within the field of contemporary photography. It is rare to find a photographer who pursues his theme without regard for extrinsic success and recognition, without compromise, but with an obsessive dedication that encompasses both life and work, and who has made it clear that there can be no distinctions made between life and work, that in fact in his case they are identical and indeed the source of the tension in his works.

With regard to photography, many still subscribe to the sterotypical view that the photographer must always stand apart from real life, that he is a passive voyeur, condemned to inactivity. Only to a certain extent can one apply to Dino Pedriali Duane Michals's comment that for some people, the camera is a vehicle through which to gain access both to people they would otherwise never be able to reach and to those, who want to use the medium itself to achieve recognition, acceptance and even admiration.

Pedriali, who was introduced to photography by Man Ray, but who learned of the power of the pictorial image from Pasolini, is quite familiar with the "Ragazzi di Vita", immortalized by the poet in literature. Their portraits, however, are his own creation. They are not the products of detached observation, as he, too, is from the Borgate, the Roman suburbs – and is in daily contact with them.

Dino Pedriali's photography becomes part of a continuing dialog conducted not via the medium of the spoken word but as an act of social acceptance with respect to these outsiders for whom looks and gestures are more significant than words.

Diane Arbus has said that in her view the subject of her photographs was always more important than the picture itself and considerably more complex as well. As important as this statement is, with reference to the limitations of the pictorial image in particular, the fundamental fact remains that for both Arbus and Pedriali this idea is very closely bound up with the viewer's reception of the photograph.

The term "model", traditionally and commonly used in connection with representations of the nude figure, is inaccurate in Pedriali's case. The bodies of those represented in these photographs do not possess the character of objects (as they very well may in their own private lives, many of them being prostitutes, street people and addicts); they are not, in fact, represented at all, for they present themselves. They demonstrate a strong sense of their own corporeal nature and a personal pride in their bodies. Even when they assume poses shockingly reminiscent of the body language of saints or mythological figures from 15th-18th century Italian art, they are never the victims of sophisticated studio photography. Pedriali takes them from the streets, undresses them and "creates" them. He consummates a process of conception in having them approach us from the depths of an impenetrable darkness, a darkness into which they seem to disappear at the next moment as if melting into the nocturnal shadows of metropolitan Rome.

"Creare il senso della vita nella fotografia" is Pedriali's motto: to present life in its full sensual intensity, but to give it a historical depth that makes figures of a Caravaggio, a Reni or a Signorelli out of the protagonists of everyday life in Rome, whom we ourselves might just as easily encounter; to reproject their bodies in the images with which our centuries-old phantasies associate them. Pedriali does not stage the photographs of his subjects. His techniques themselves are simple, succinct and efficient. His own passion in making these photographs goes far beyond mere erotic fascination. It is not content to rest in genre or documentation, and certainly not in journalistic reporting, but becomes instead an act of pure poetry such as can be found only among the great photographers of our century, a poetry that nevertheless incorporates erotic fascination within itself. The bodies are neither beautified nor stylized. On the other hand, the photograph lends the figures an ideal quality we normally expect to find only in painting or sculpture. Black and white are the two provinces of this photography. As is true as well for the nakedness of the bodies, these areas are characteristic of something fundamental. For Pedriali, photography is a poetic language of fundamental images which cannot be replaced or dissolved with words.

Plates

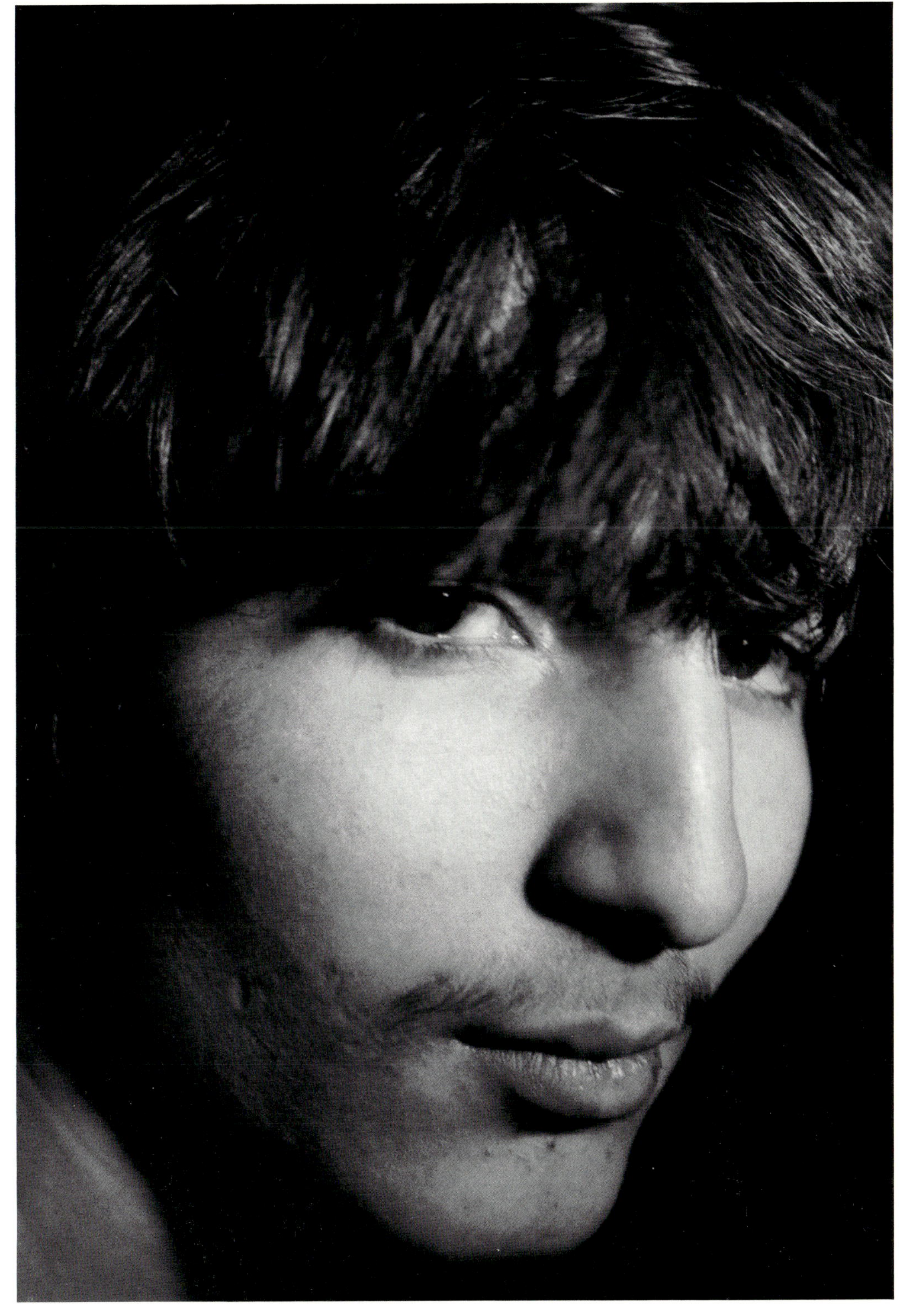

Ritratto d'un Giovane, 1981

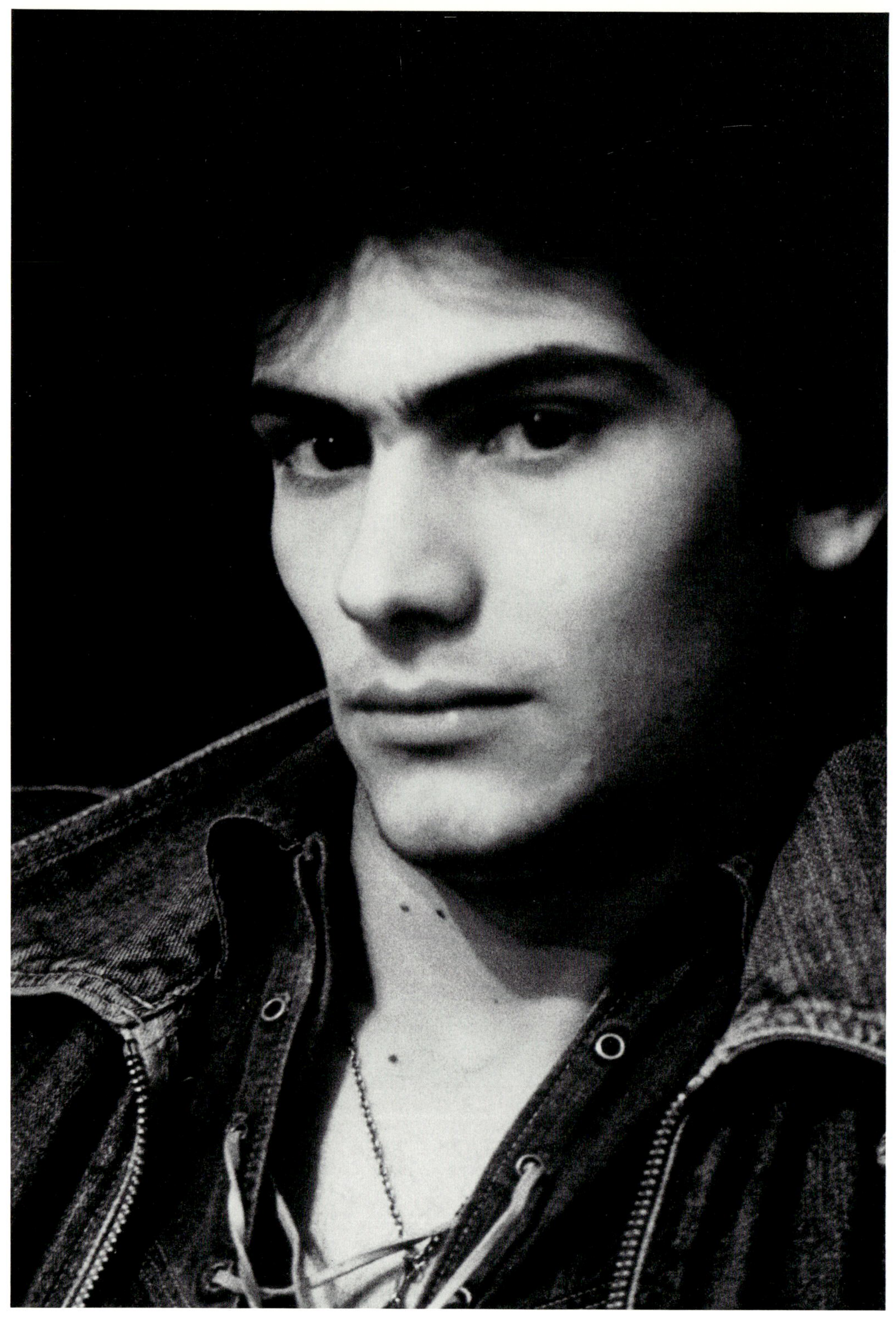

Ritratto d'un Giovane, 1978

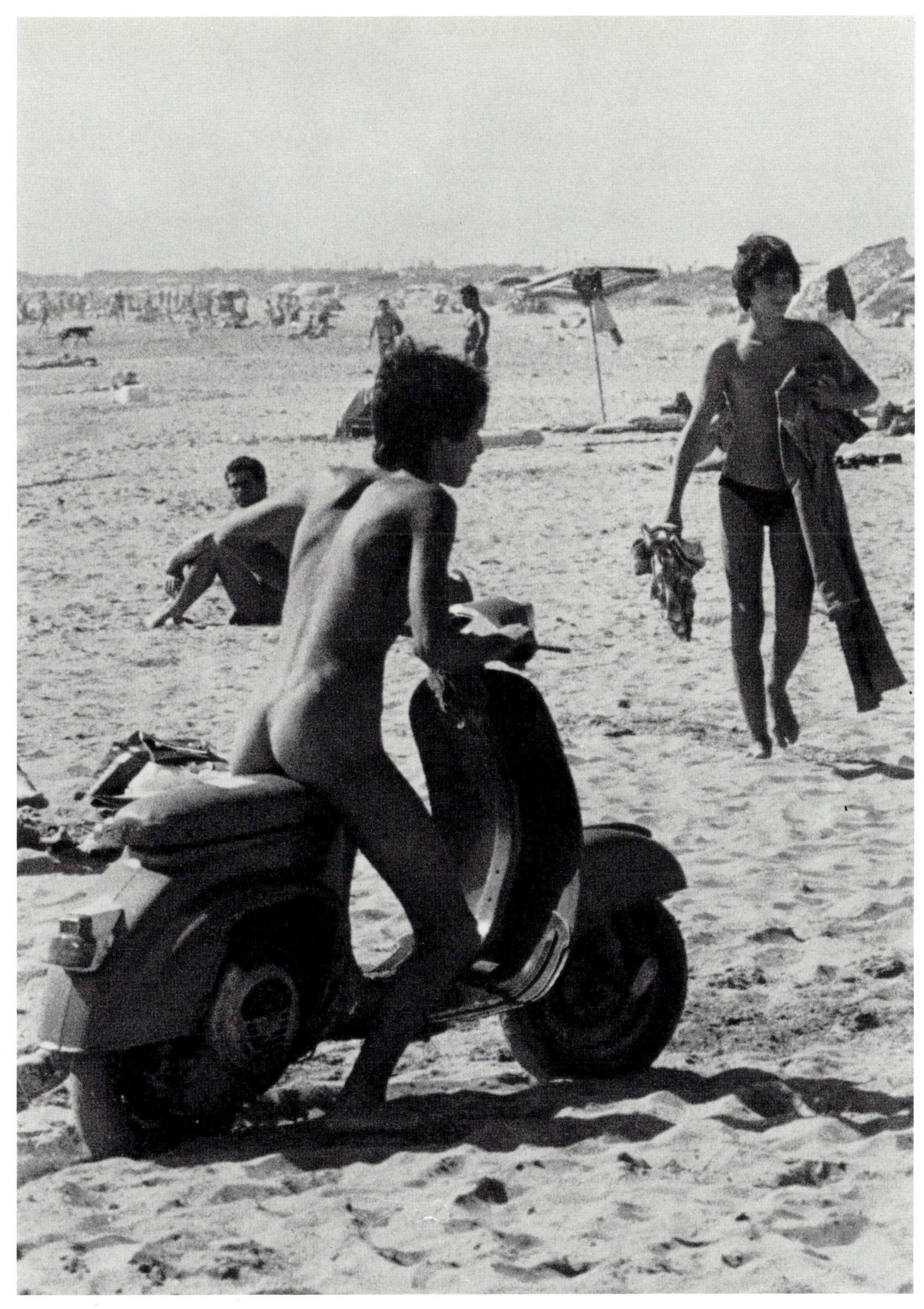

Al Buco, 1976

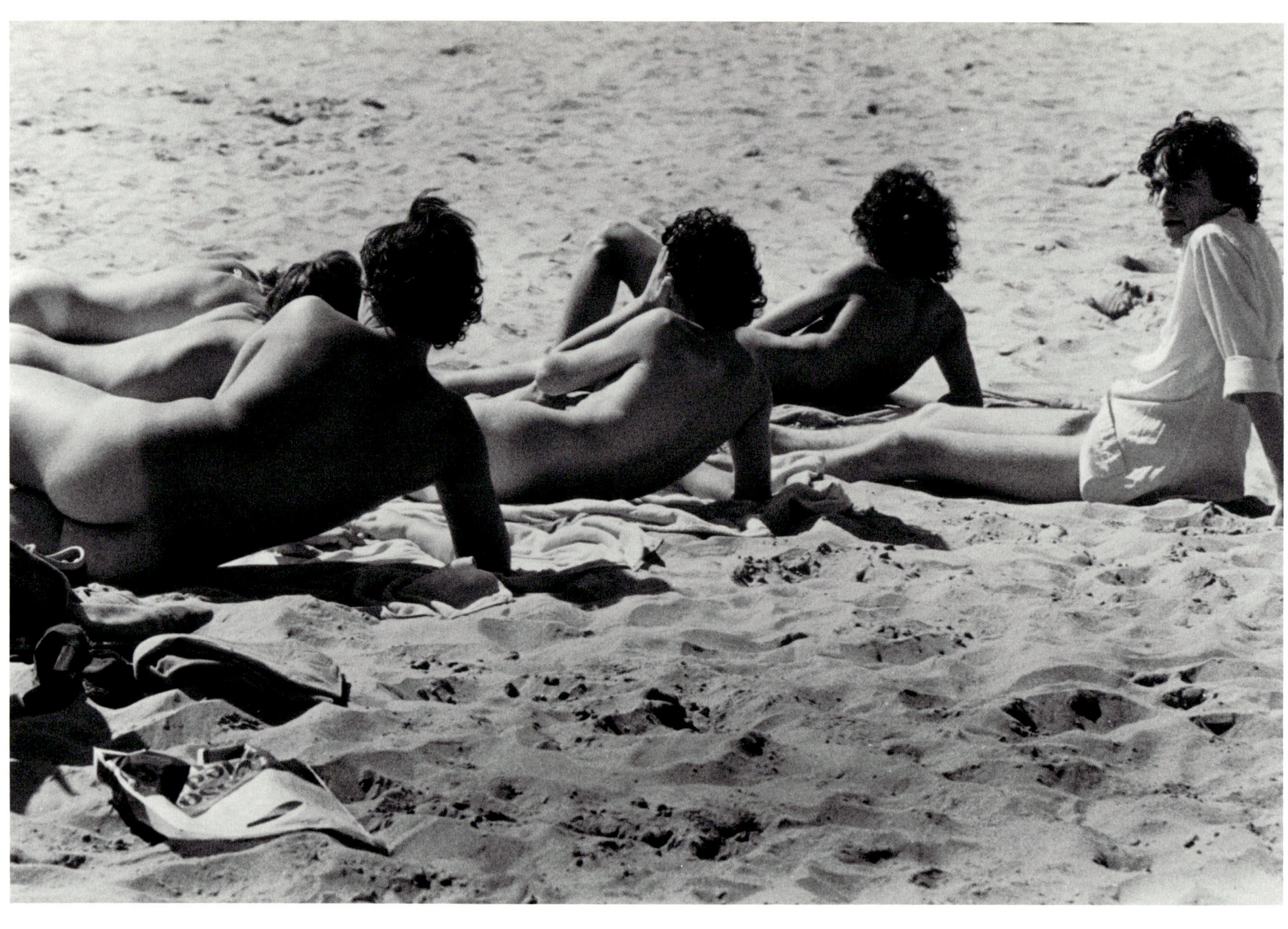

 Al Buco, 1976

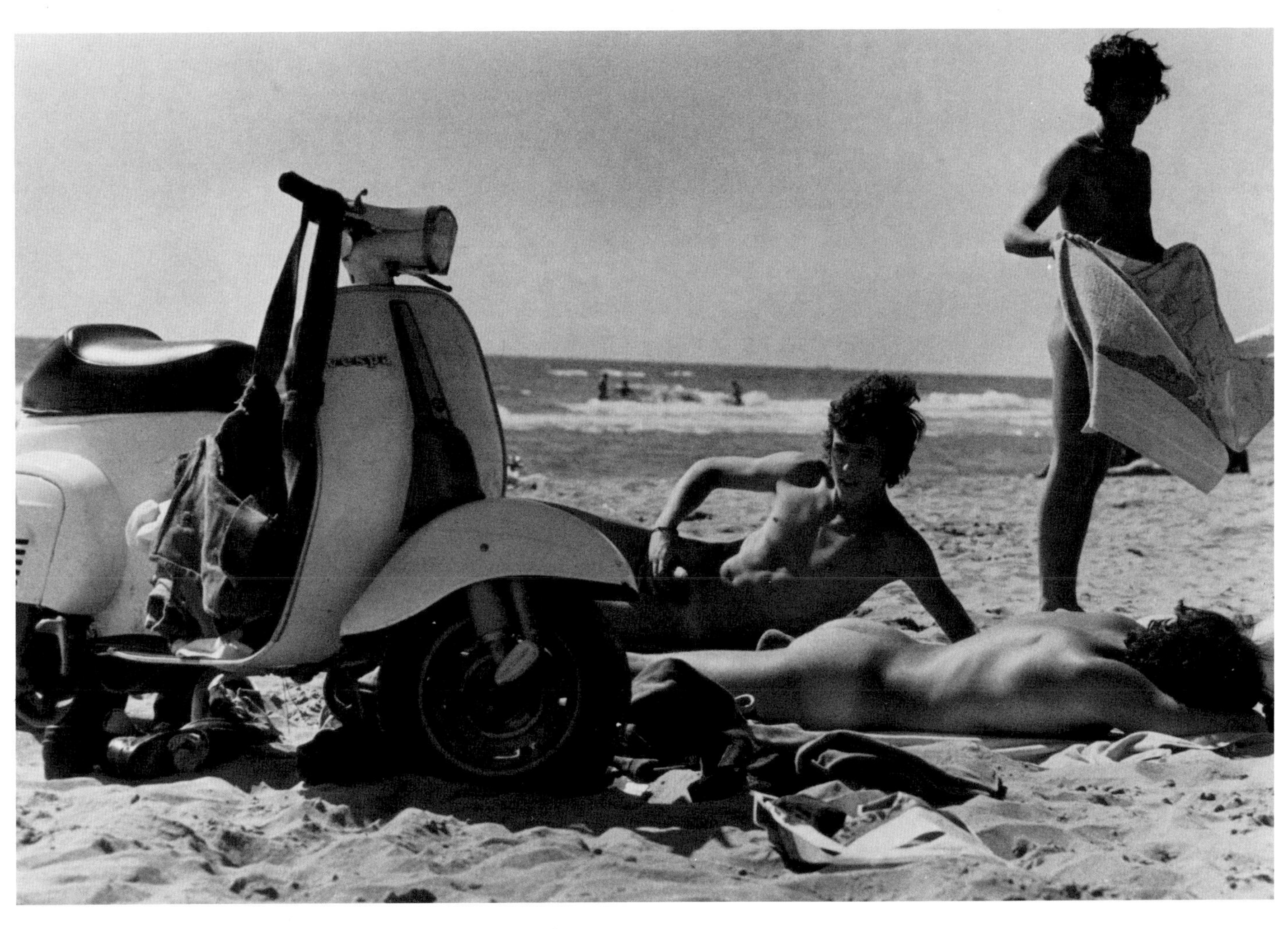

Al Buco, 1976

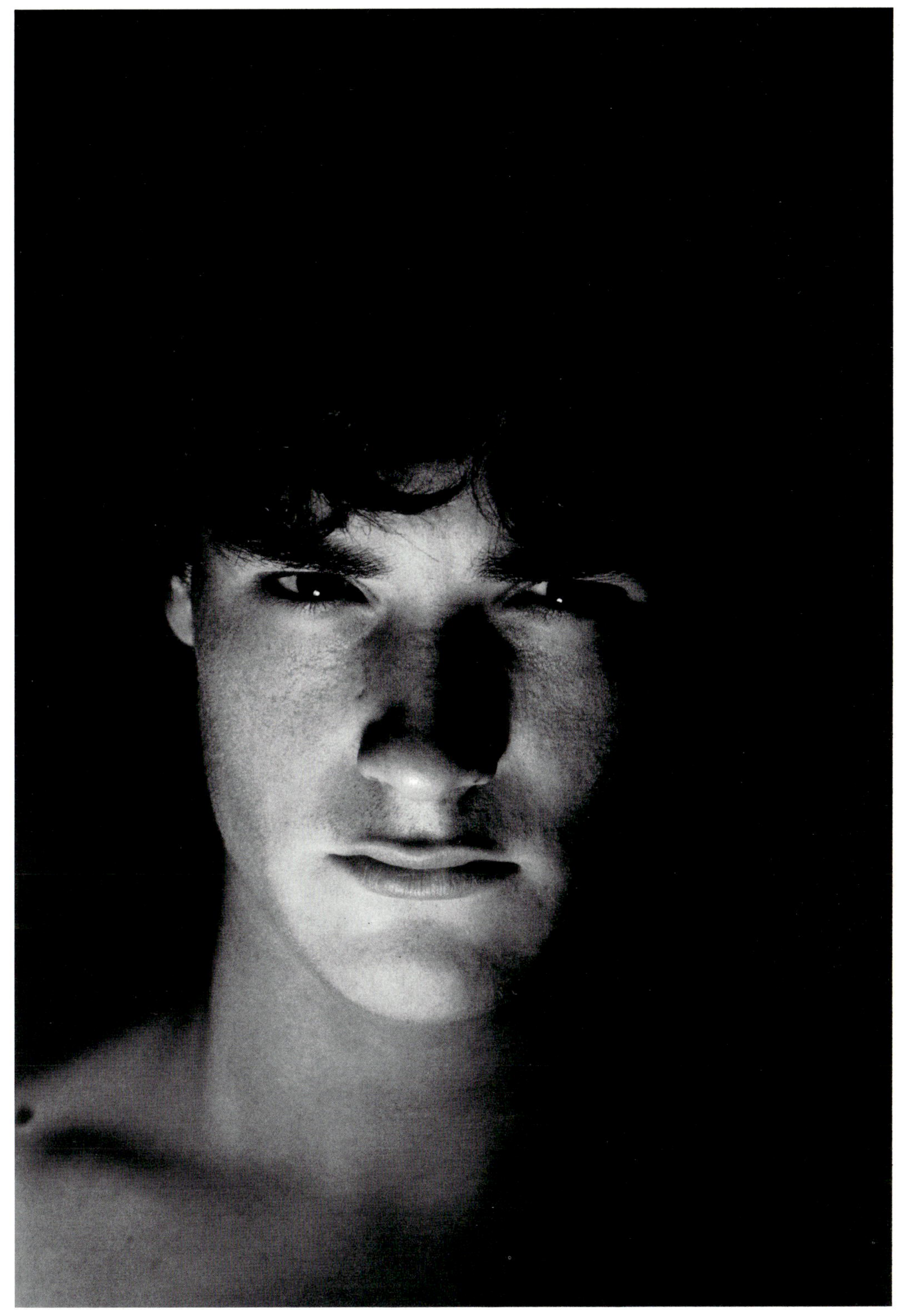

Tonino dei Ponti, 1982

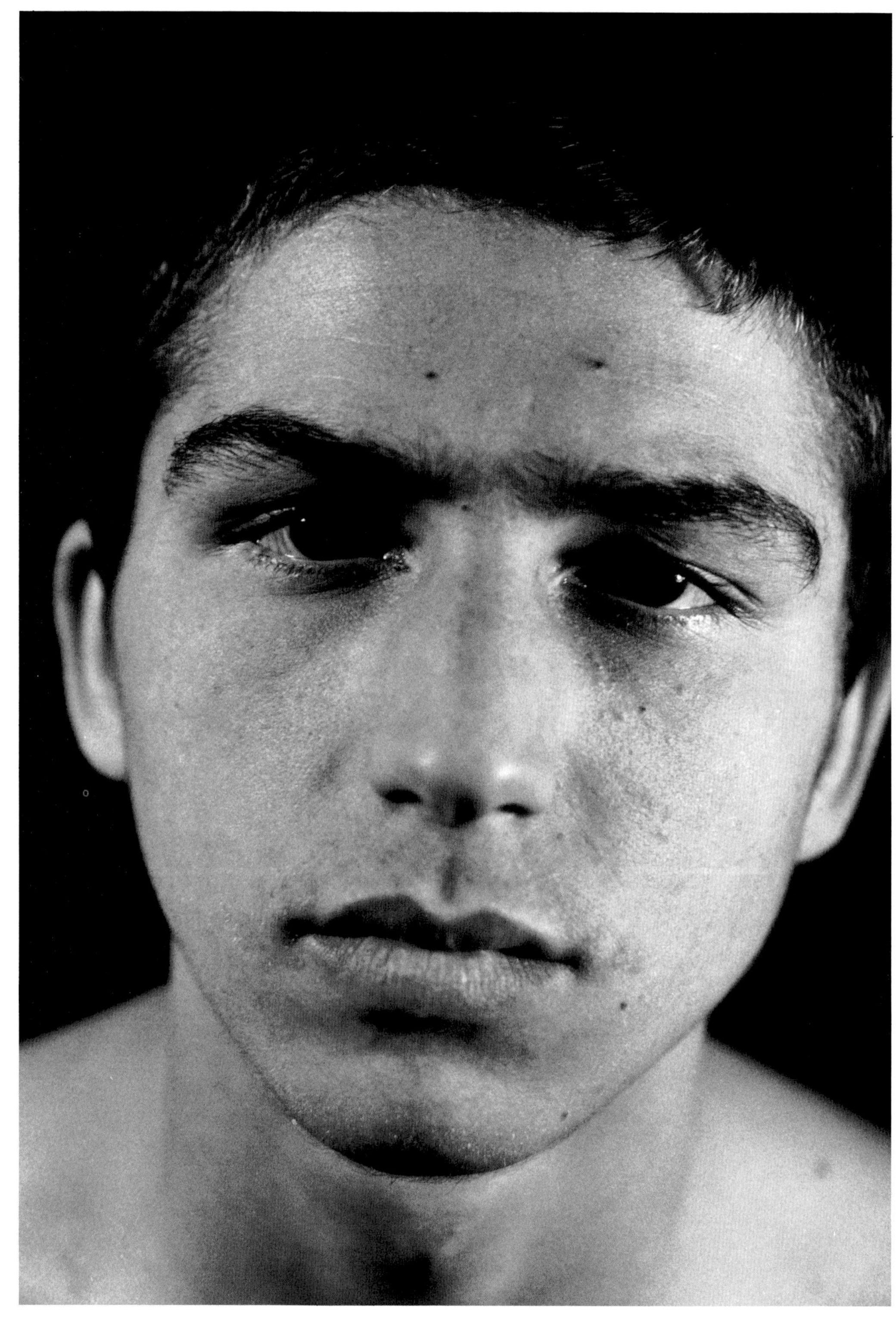

Ritratto d'un Giovane, 1981

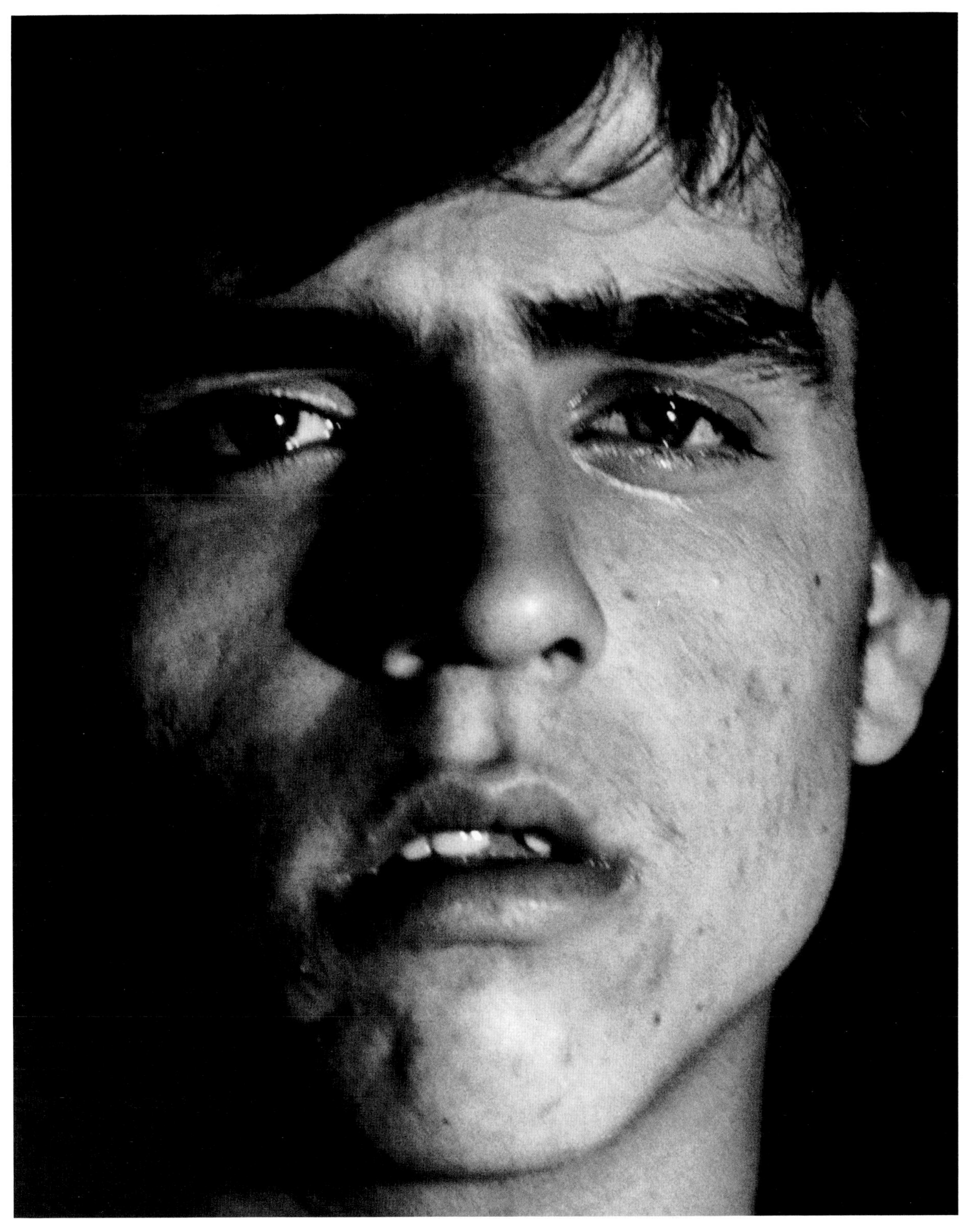

Ritratto d'un Giovane, 1977

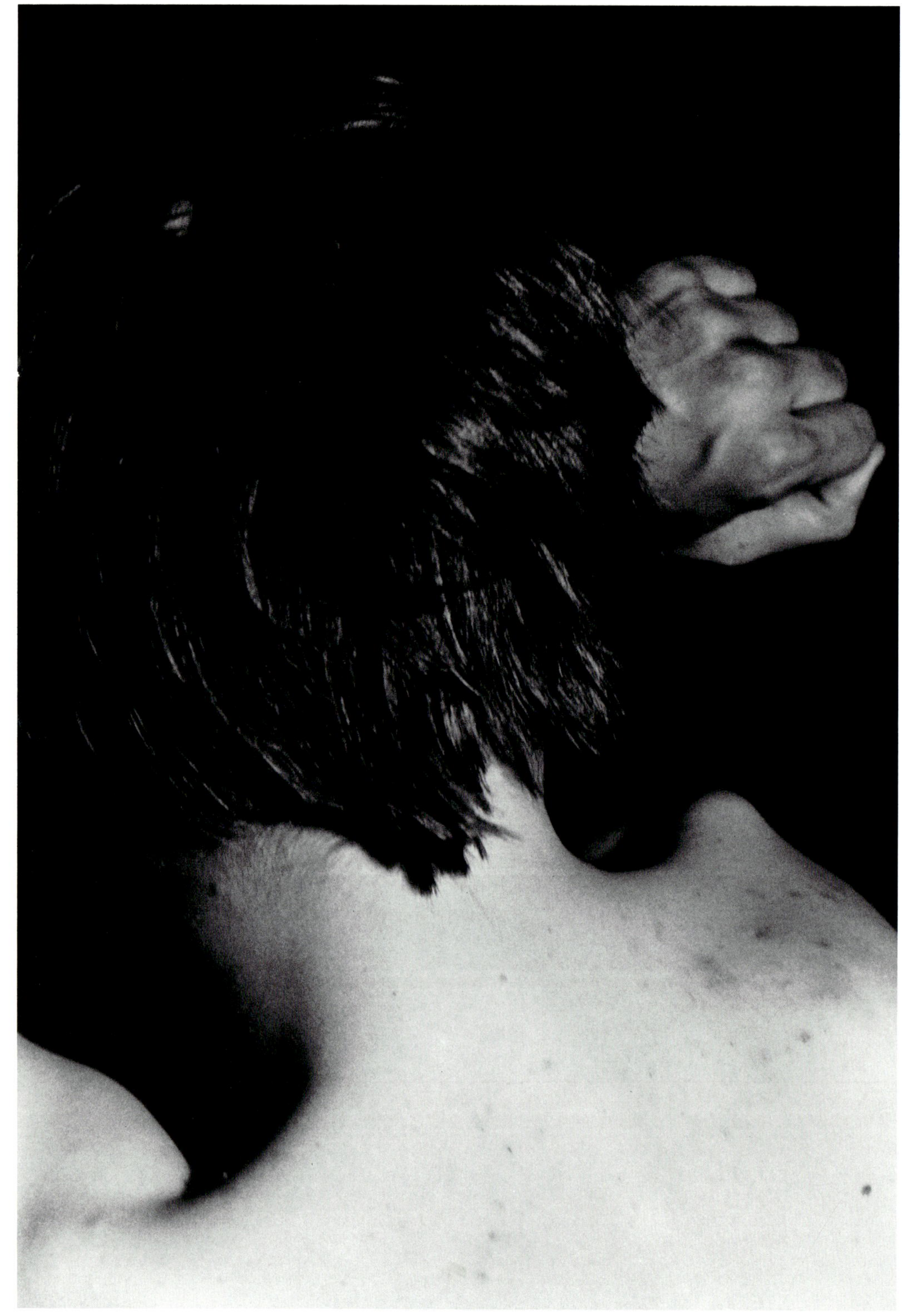

Claudio, 1980

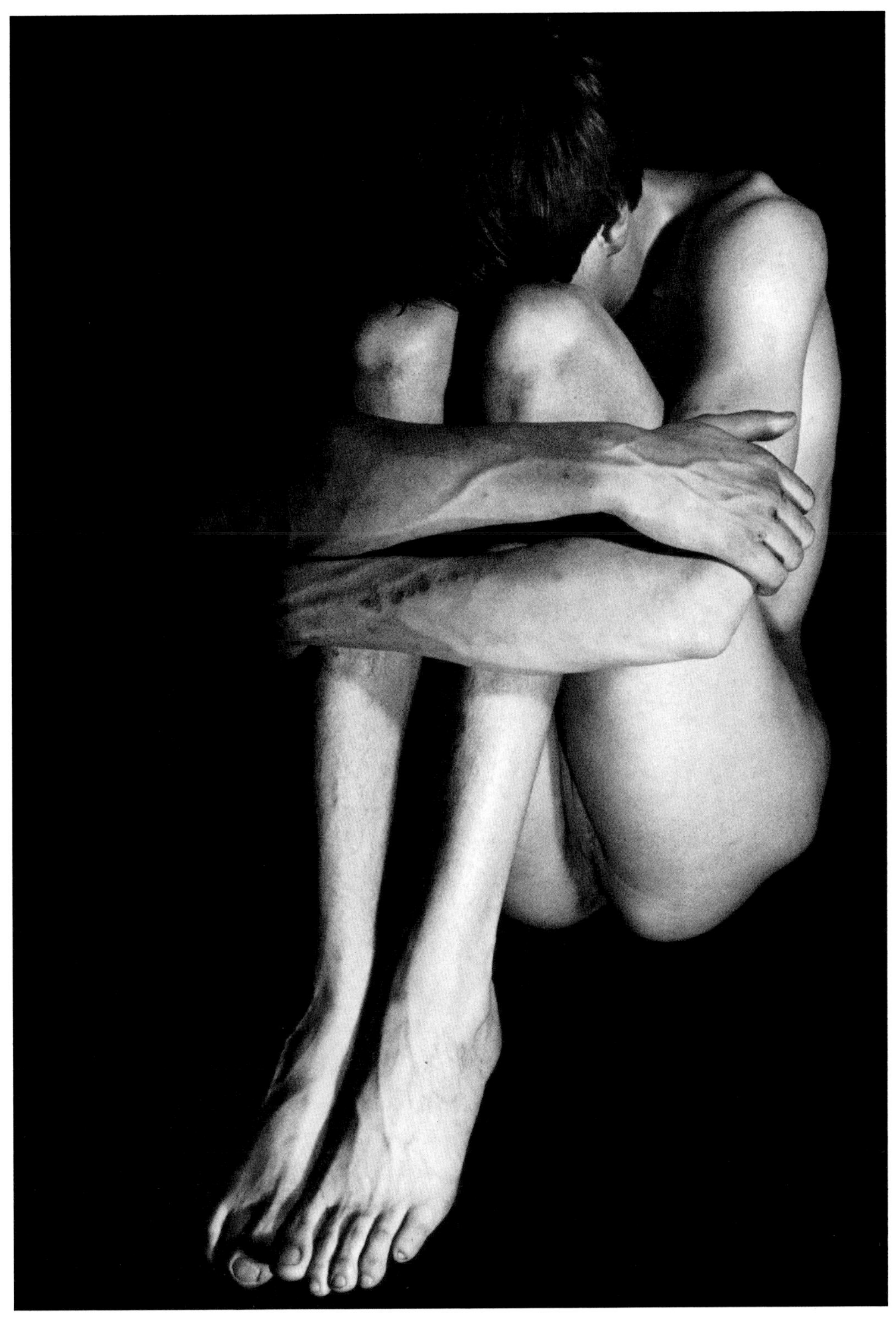

Claudio, 1980

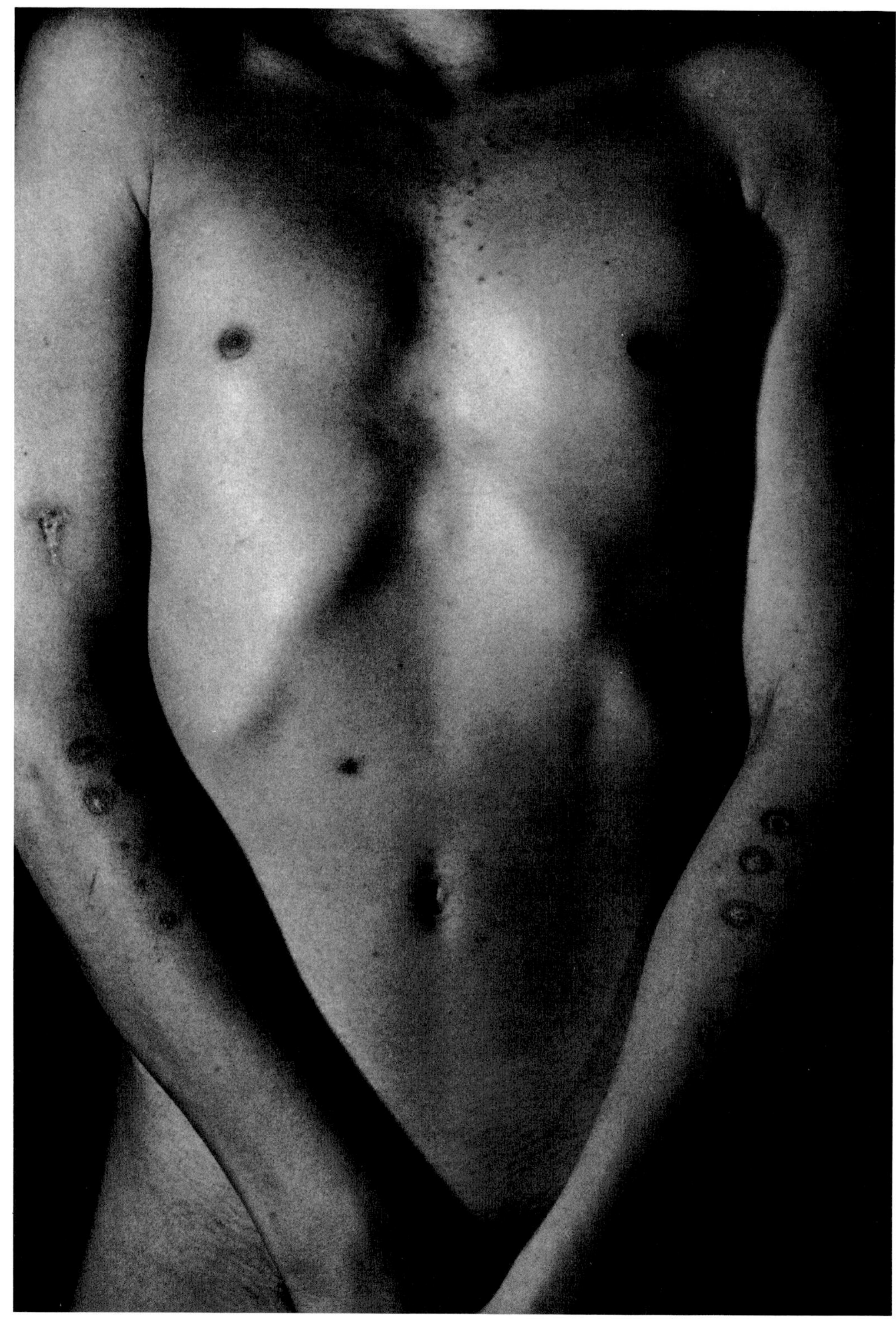

Claudio, 1980

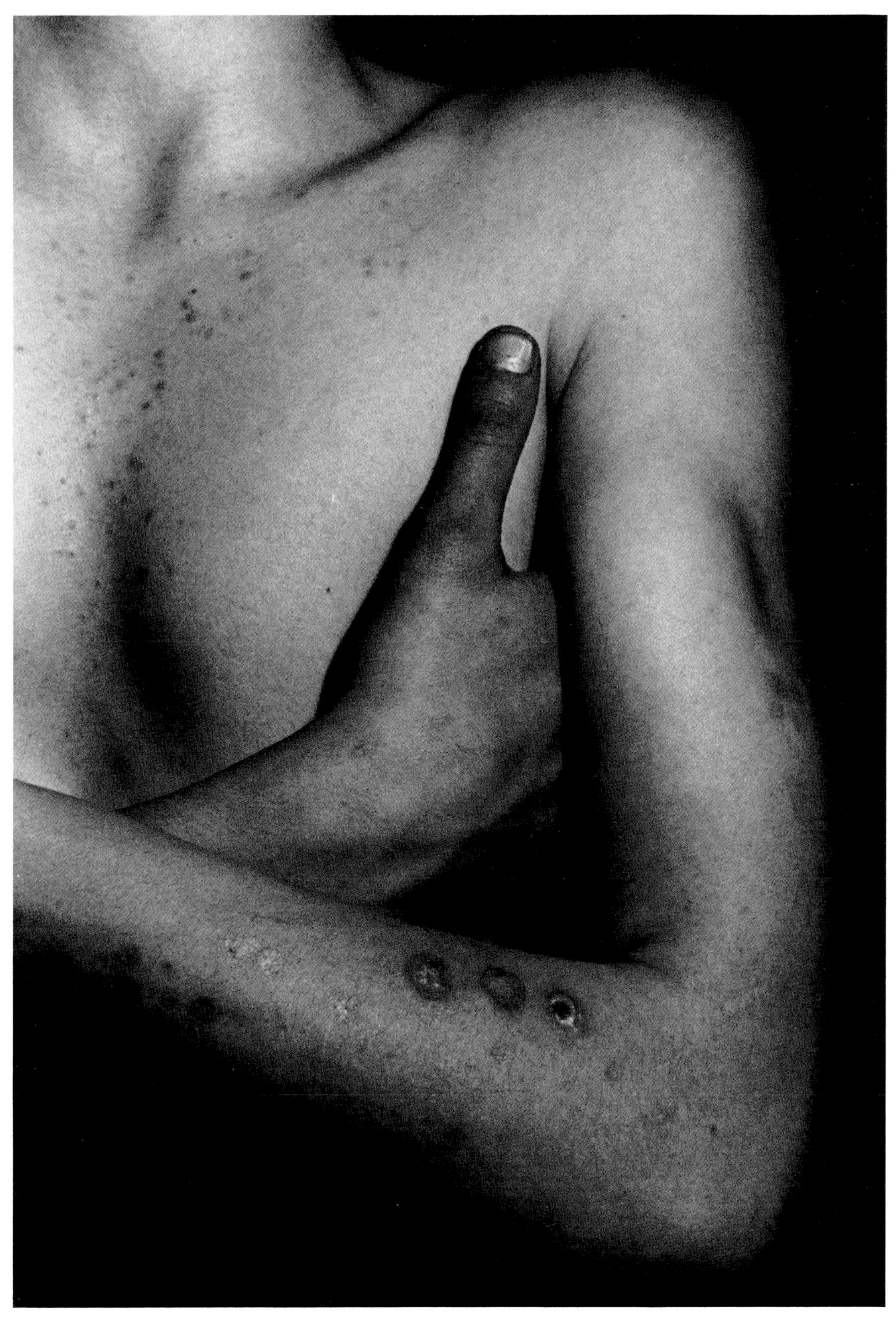

Claudio, 1980

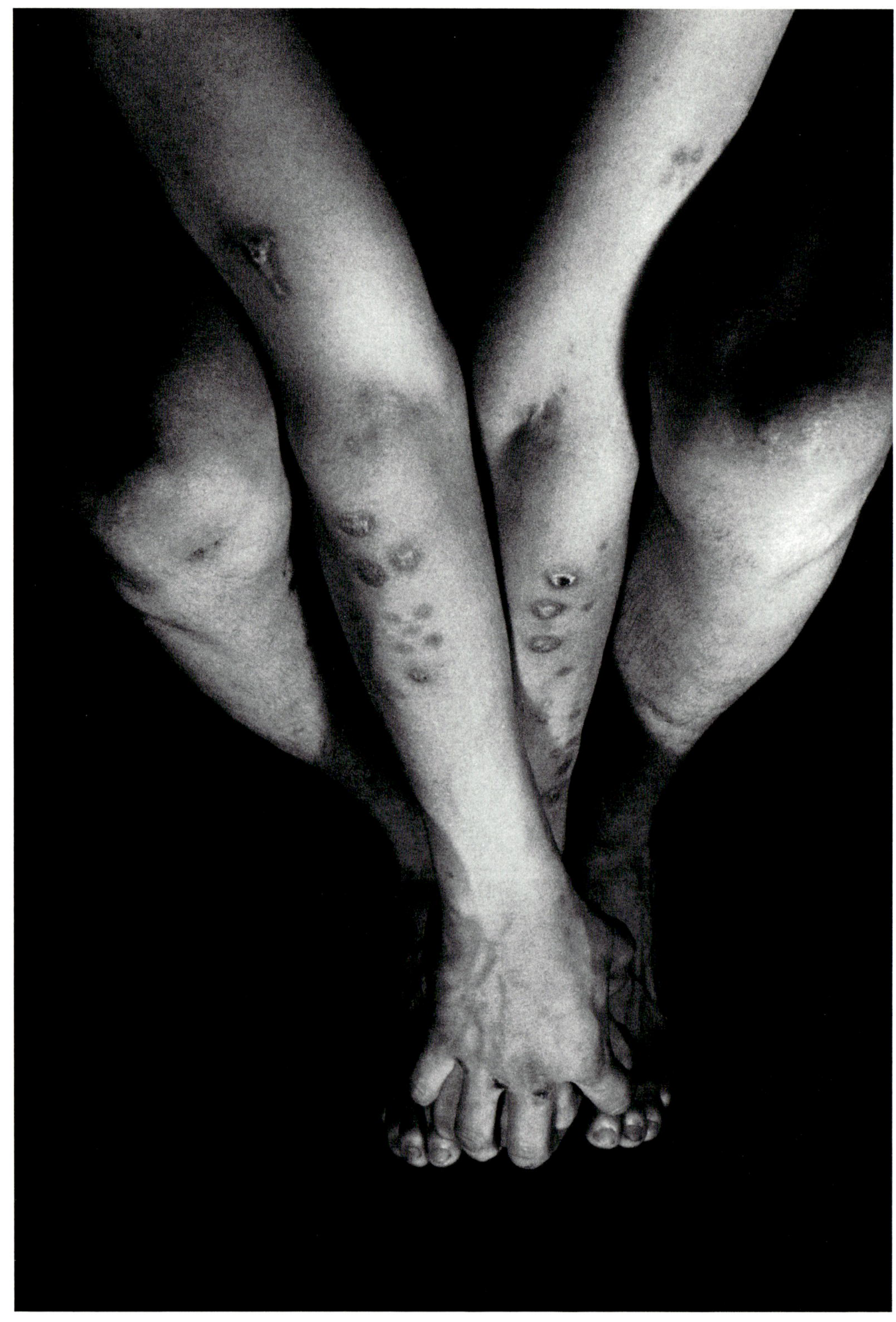

Claudio, 1980

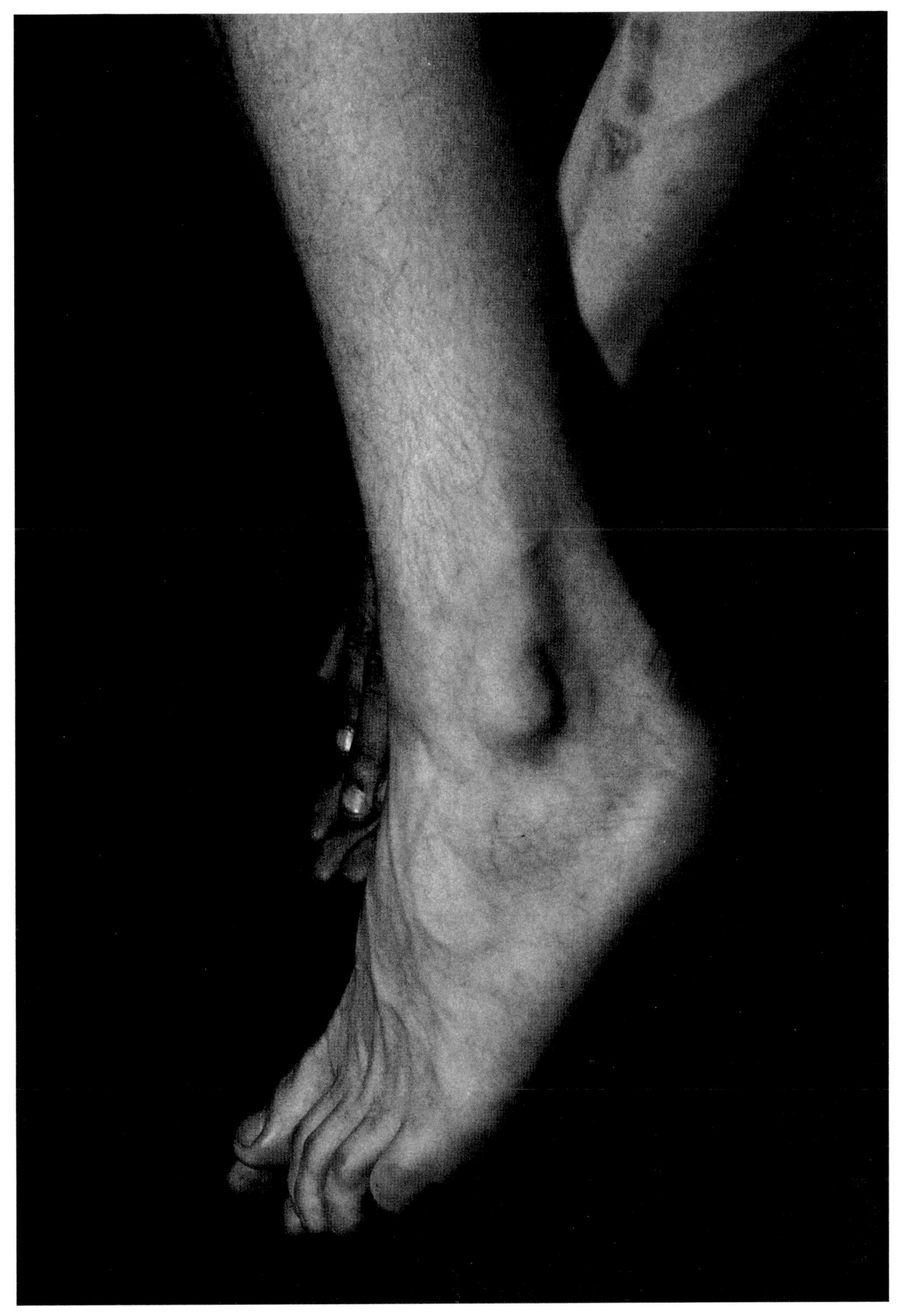

Claudio, 1980

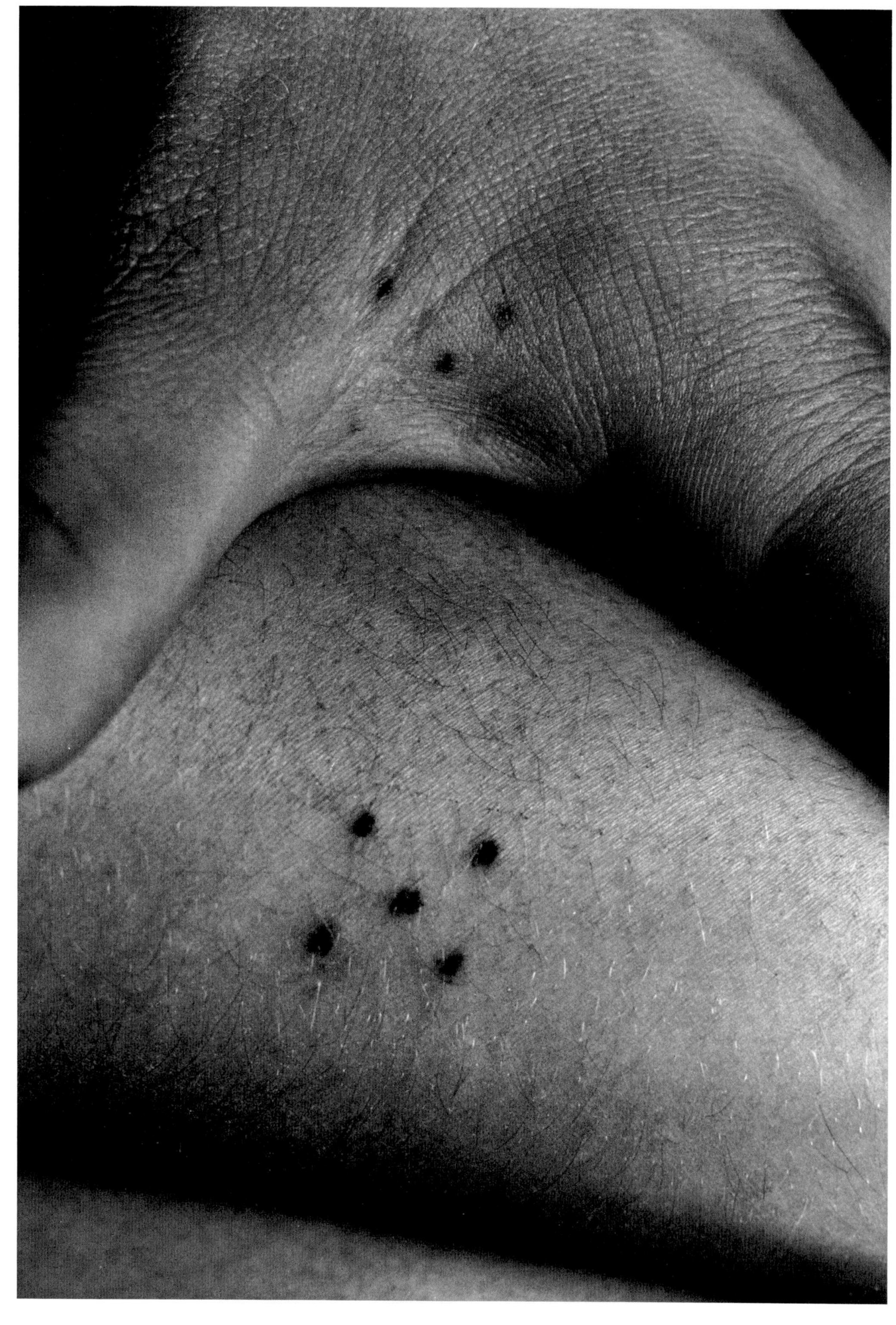

Senza Titolo, 1981

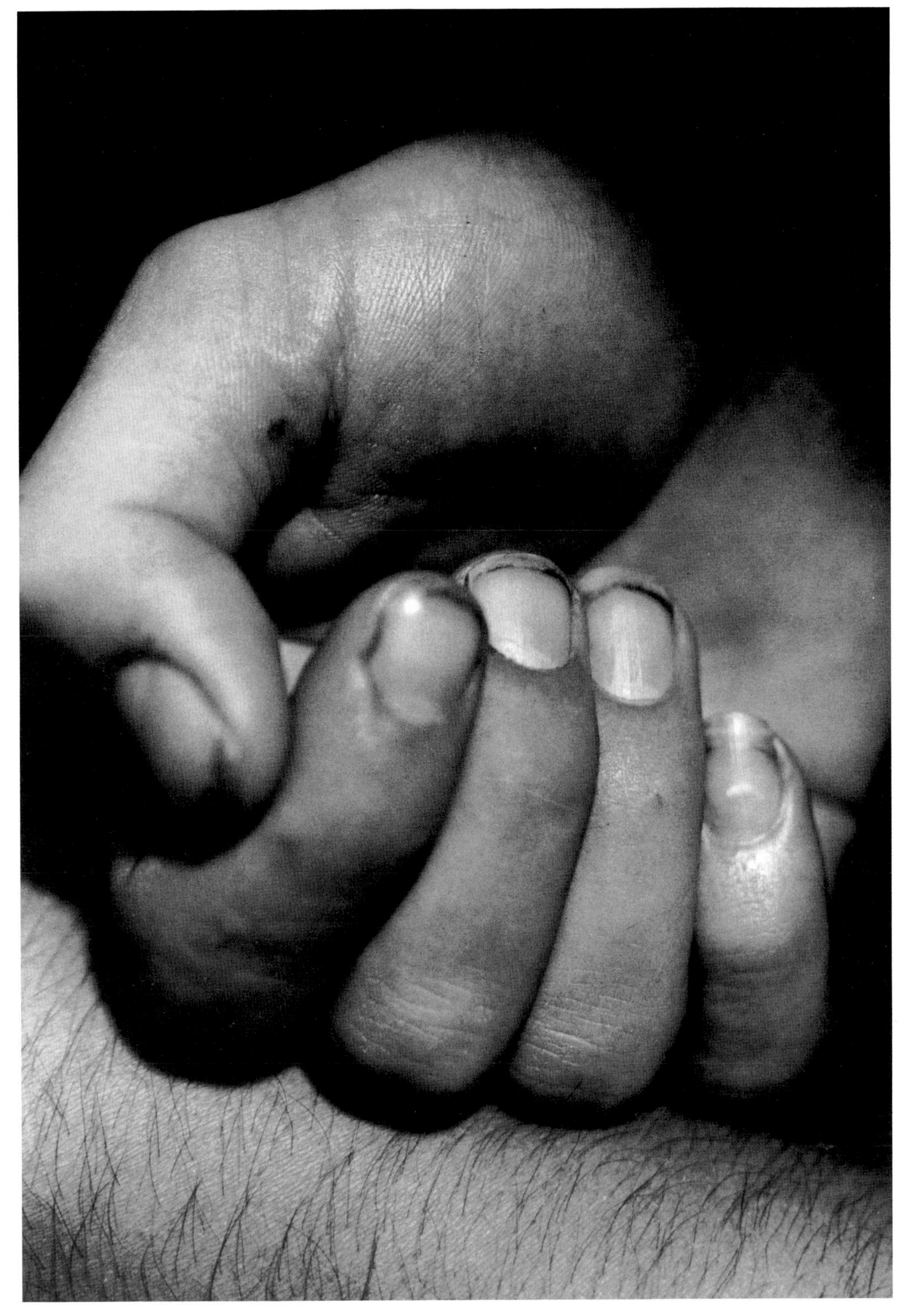

Senza Titolo, 1981

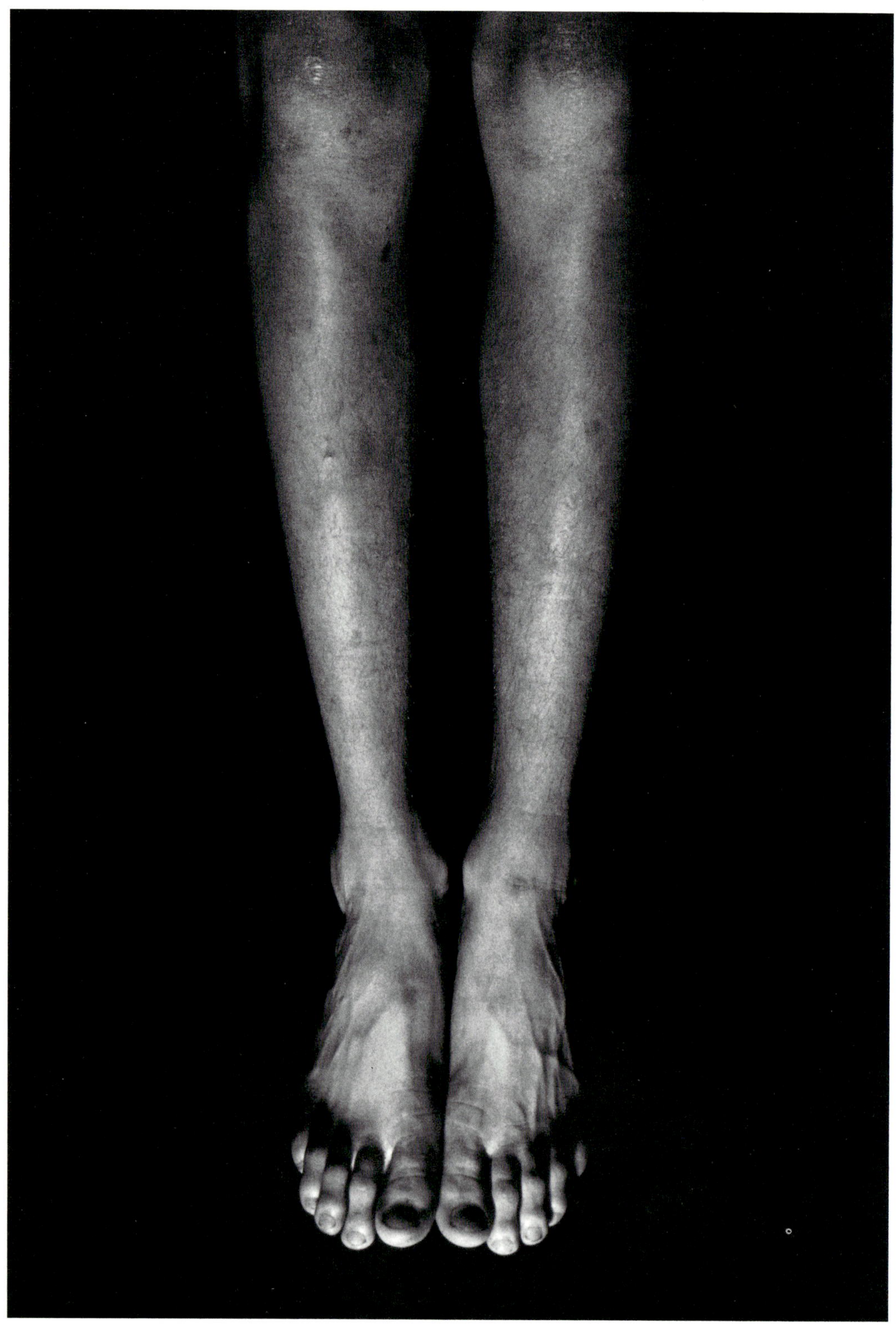

Claudio, 1980

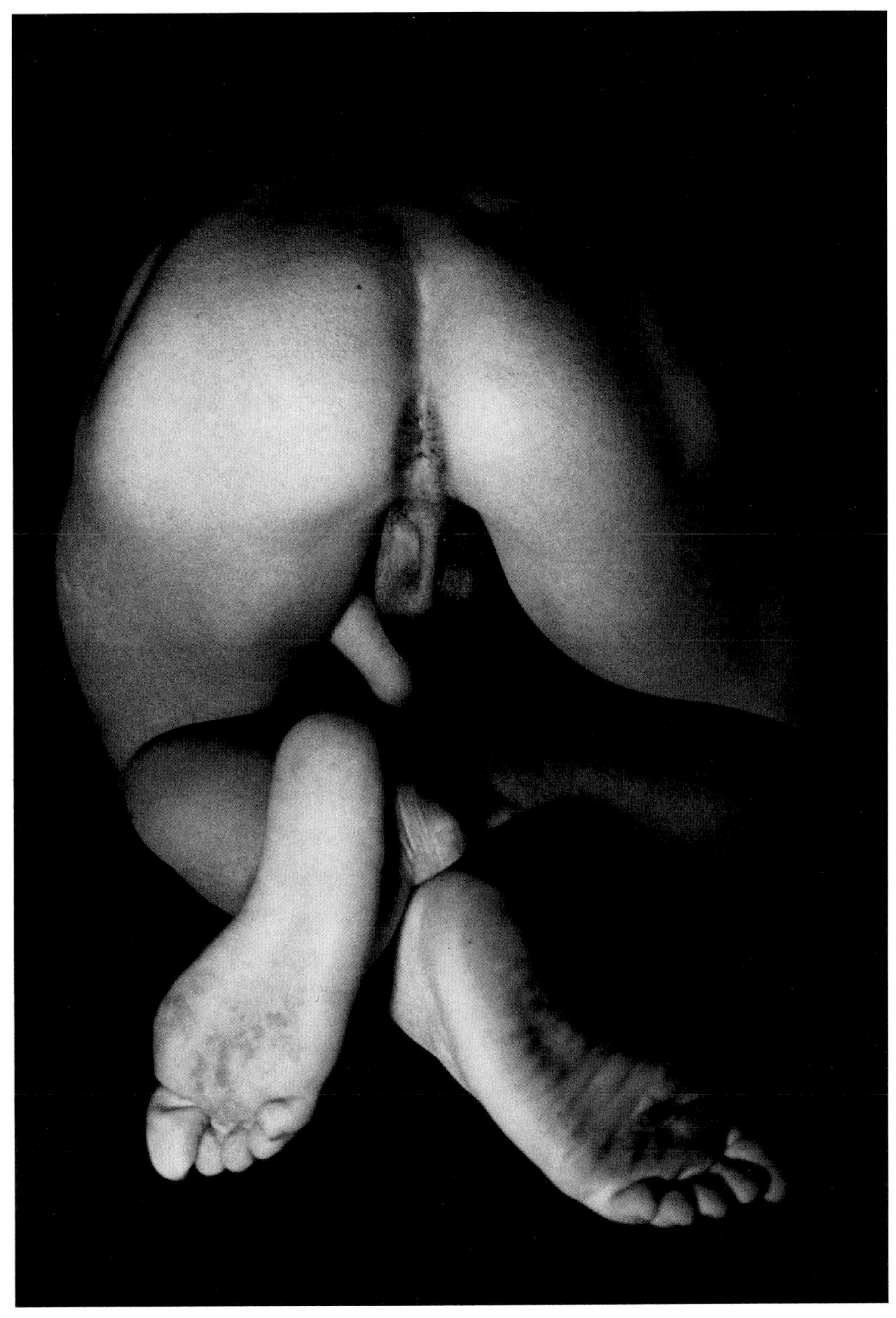

Senza Titolo, 1981

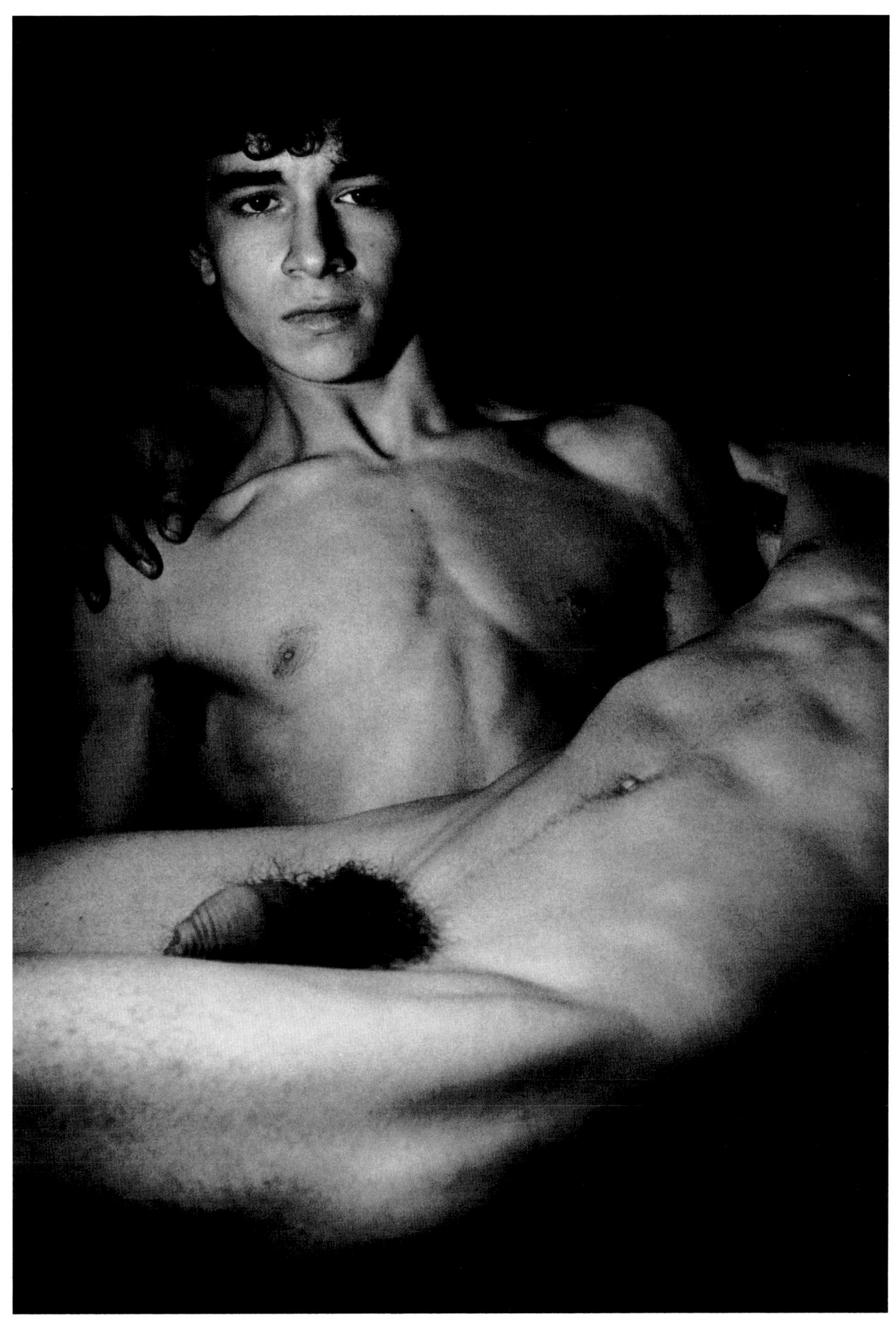

Gli Fratelli Romolo e Claudio, 1984

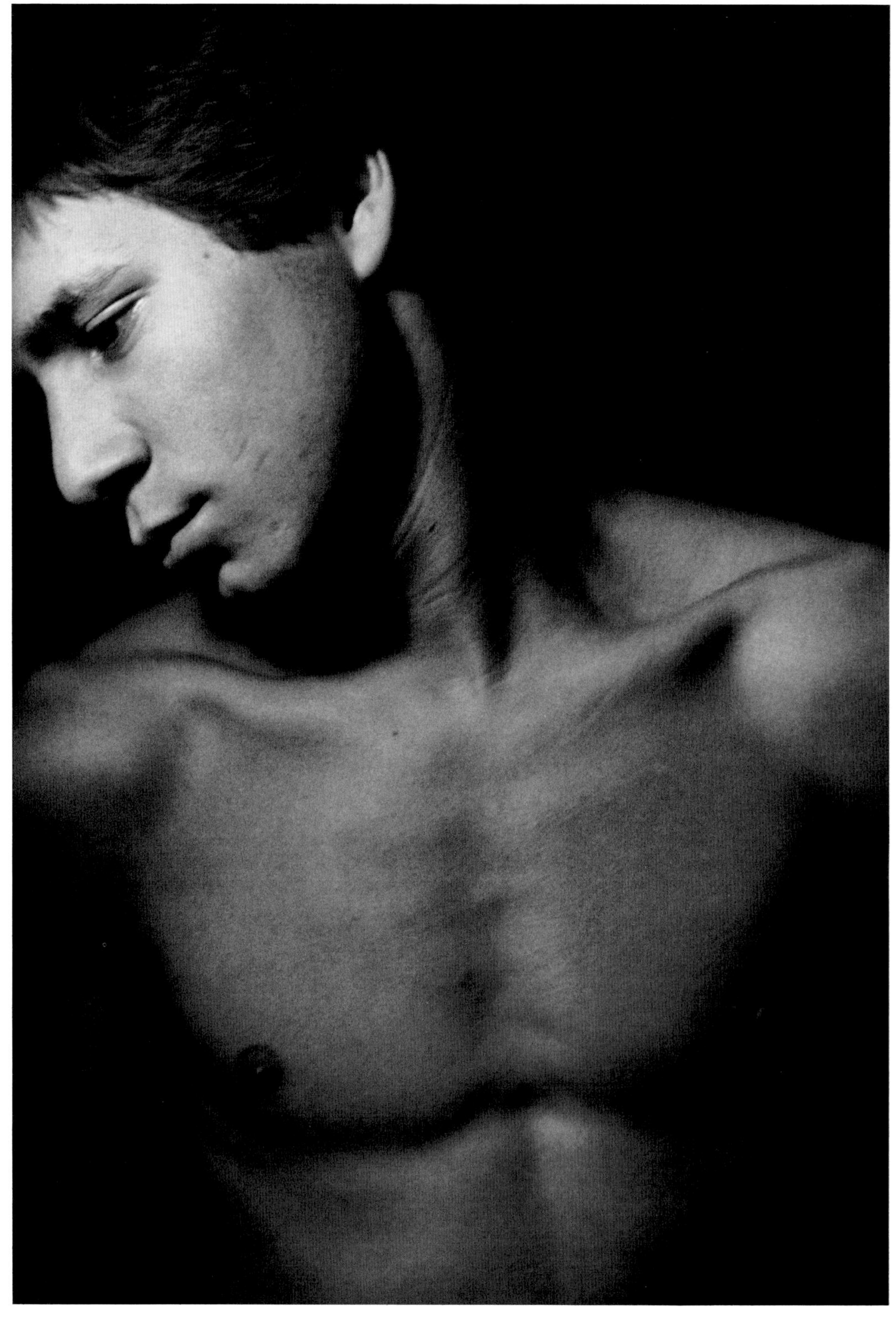

 Carmine, 1984

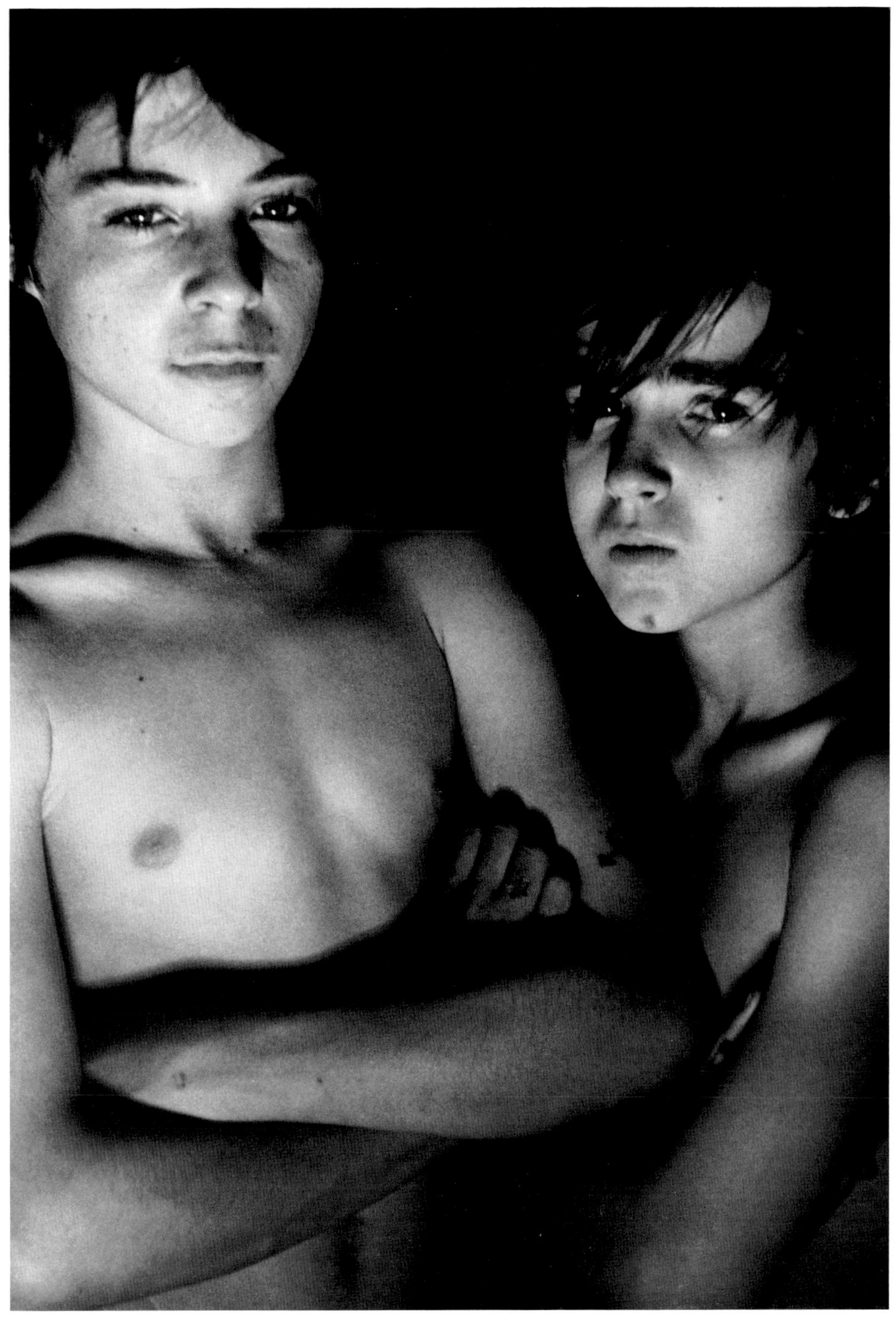

Filippo ed Antonio, 1983

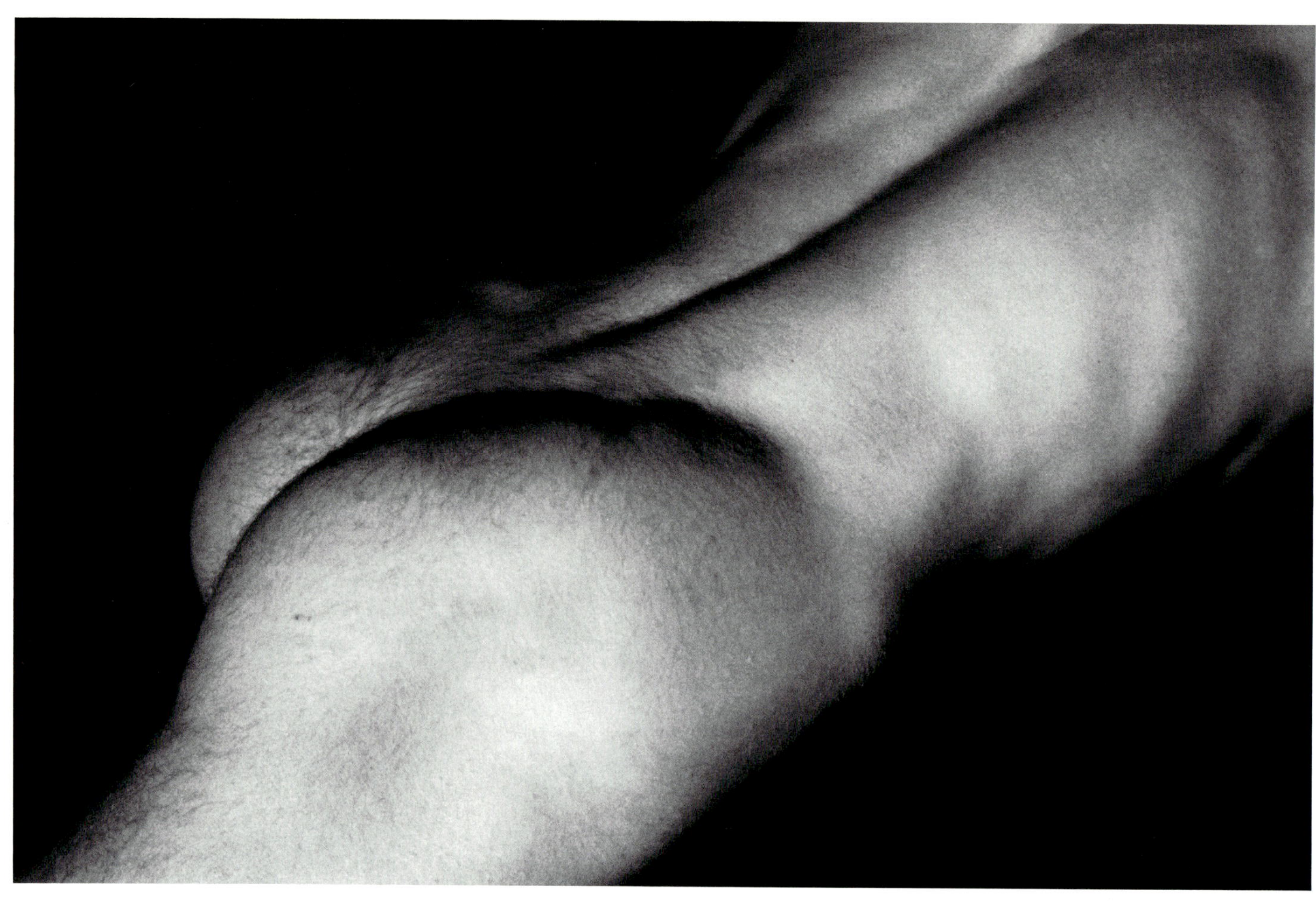

 Senza Titolo, 1981

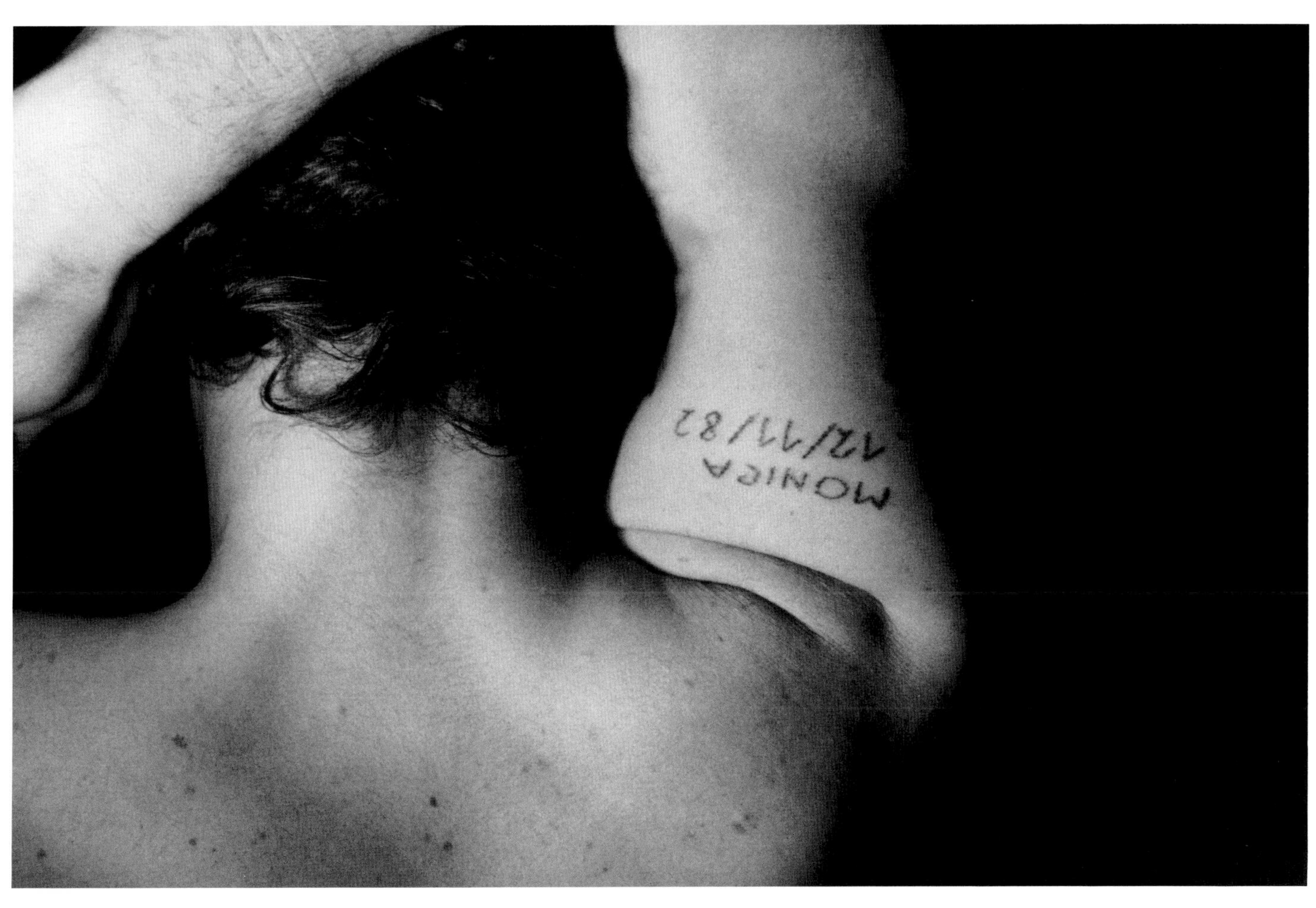

Marcello, 1984

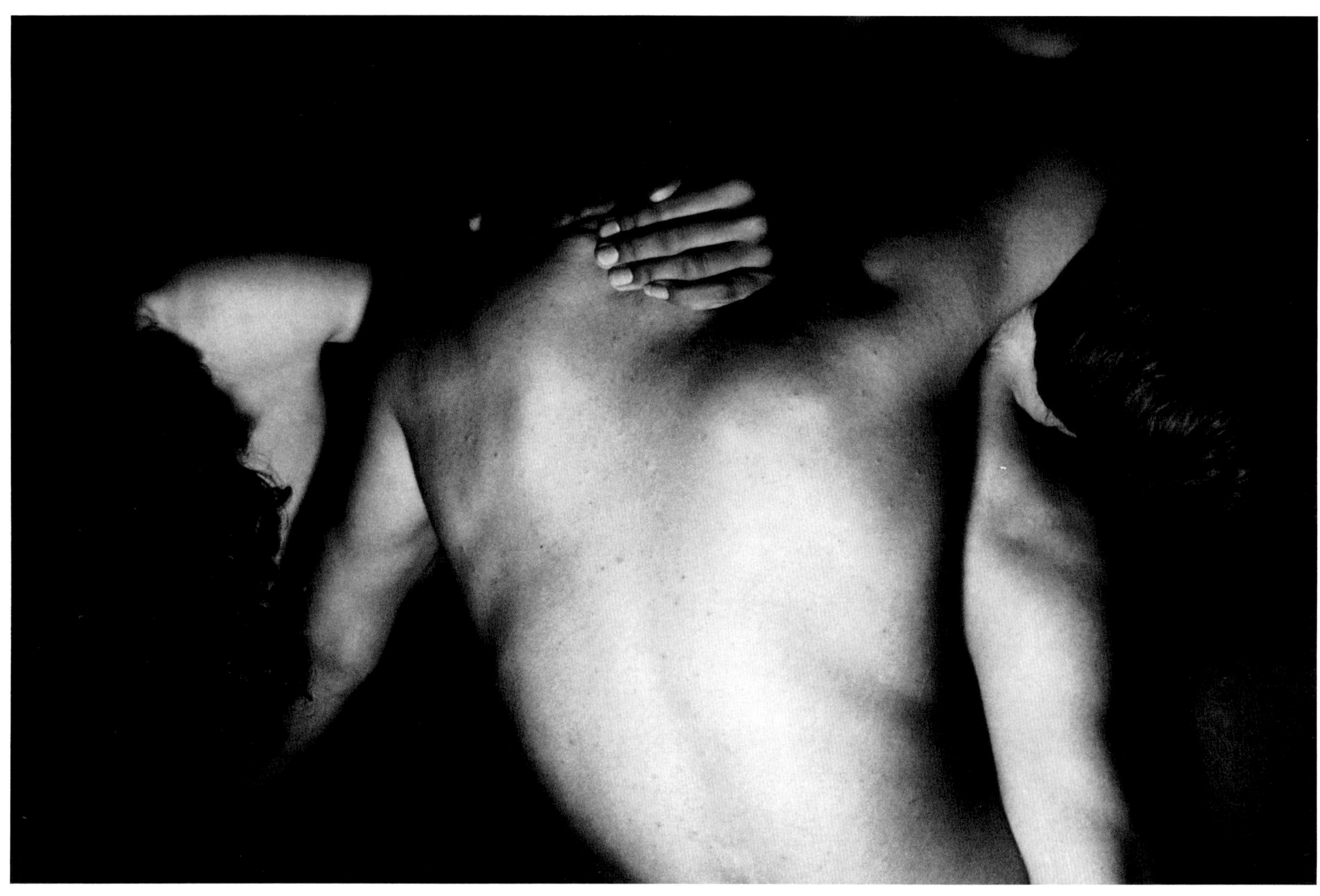

 Mio Studio di Nudo, 1984

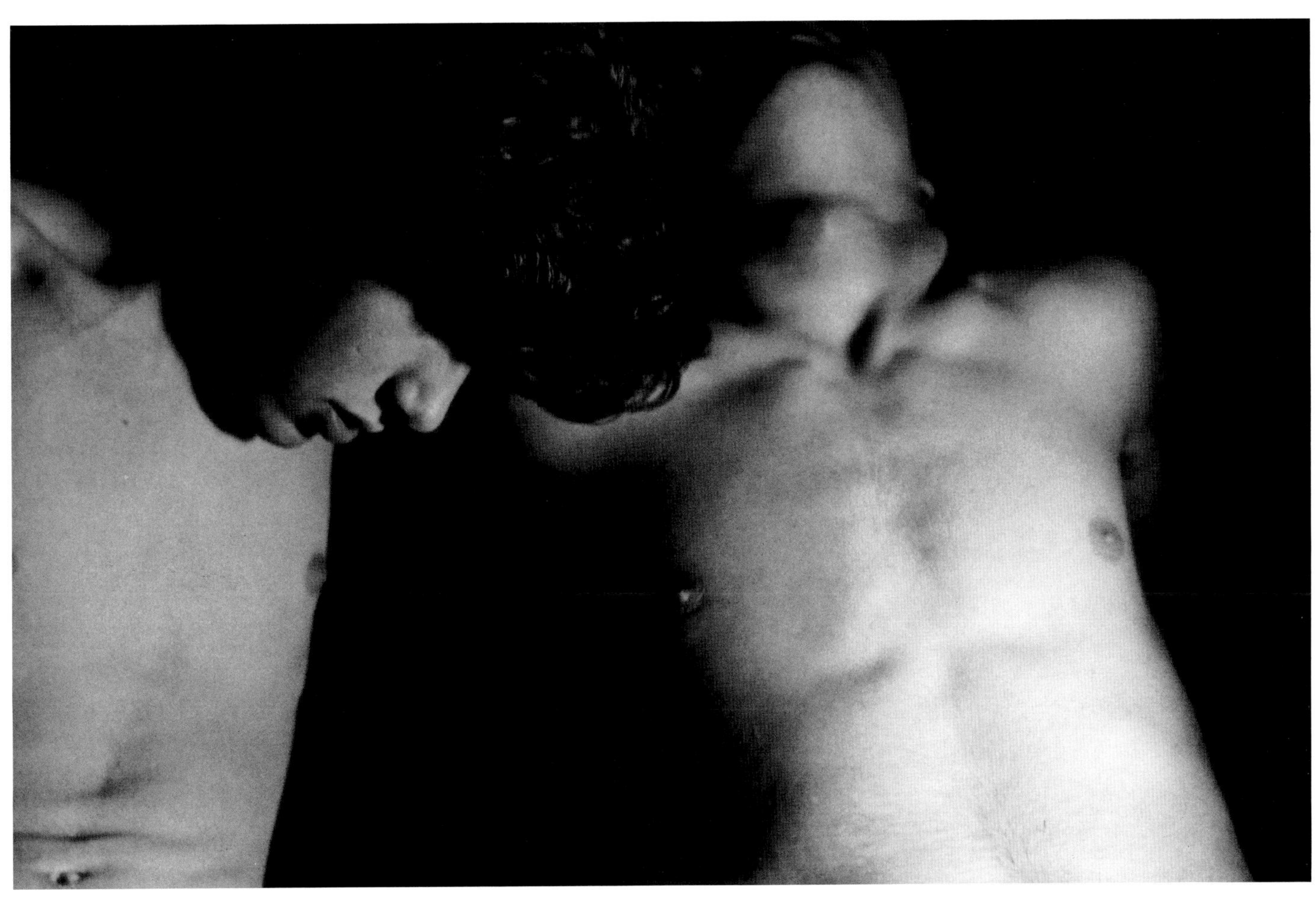

Amici del distretto, 1984

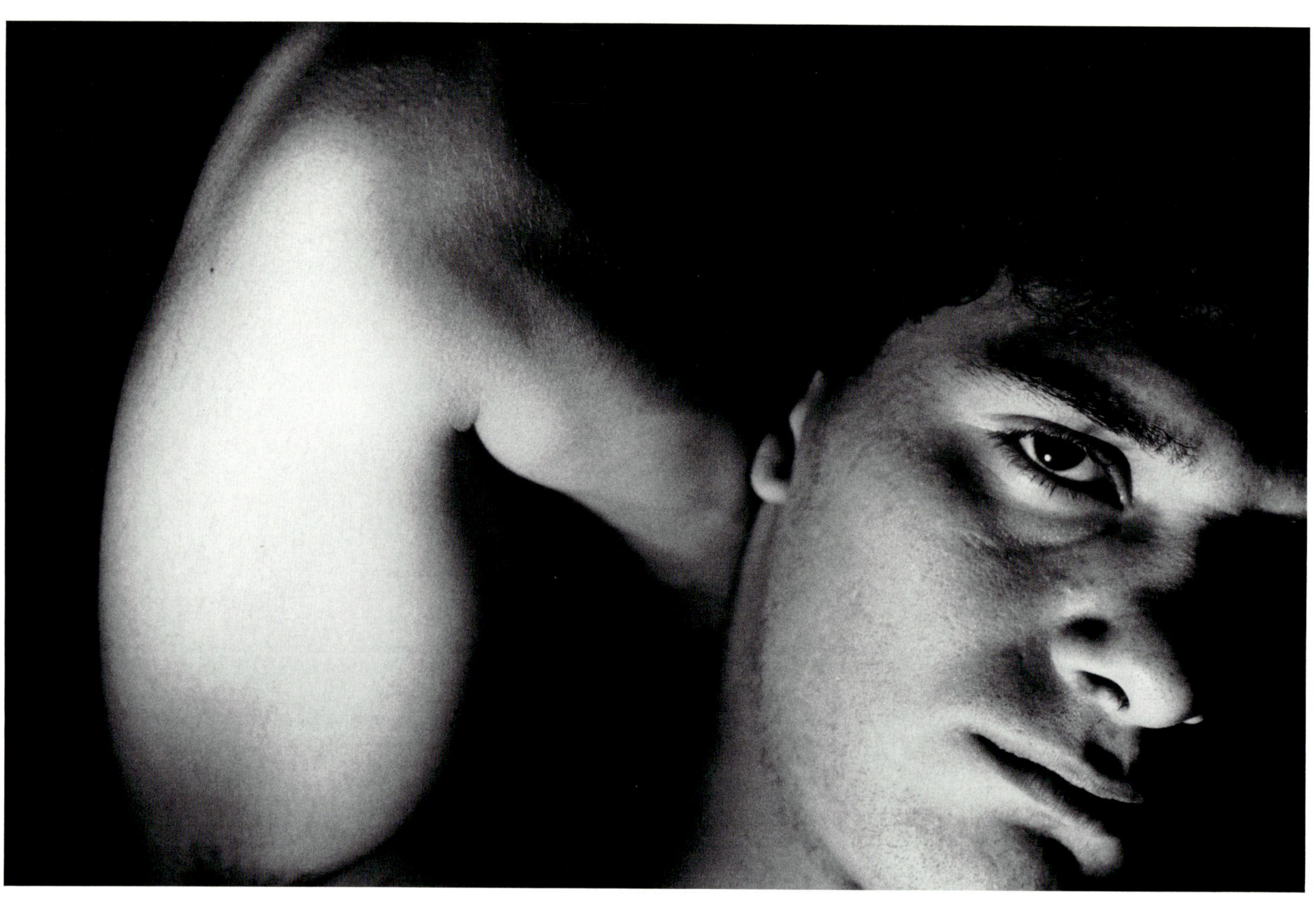

 Pasqualino, 1983

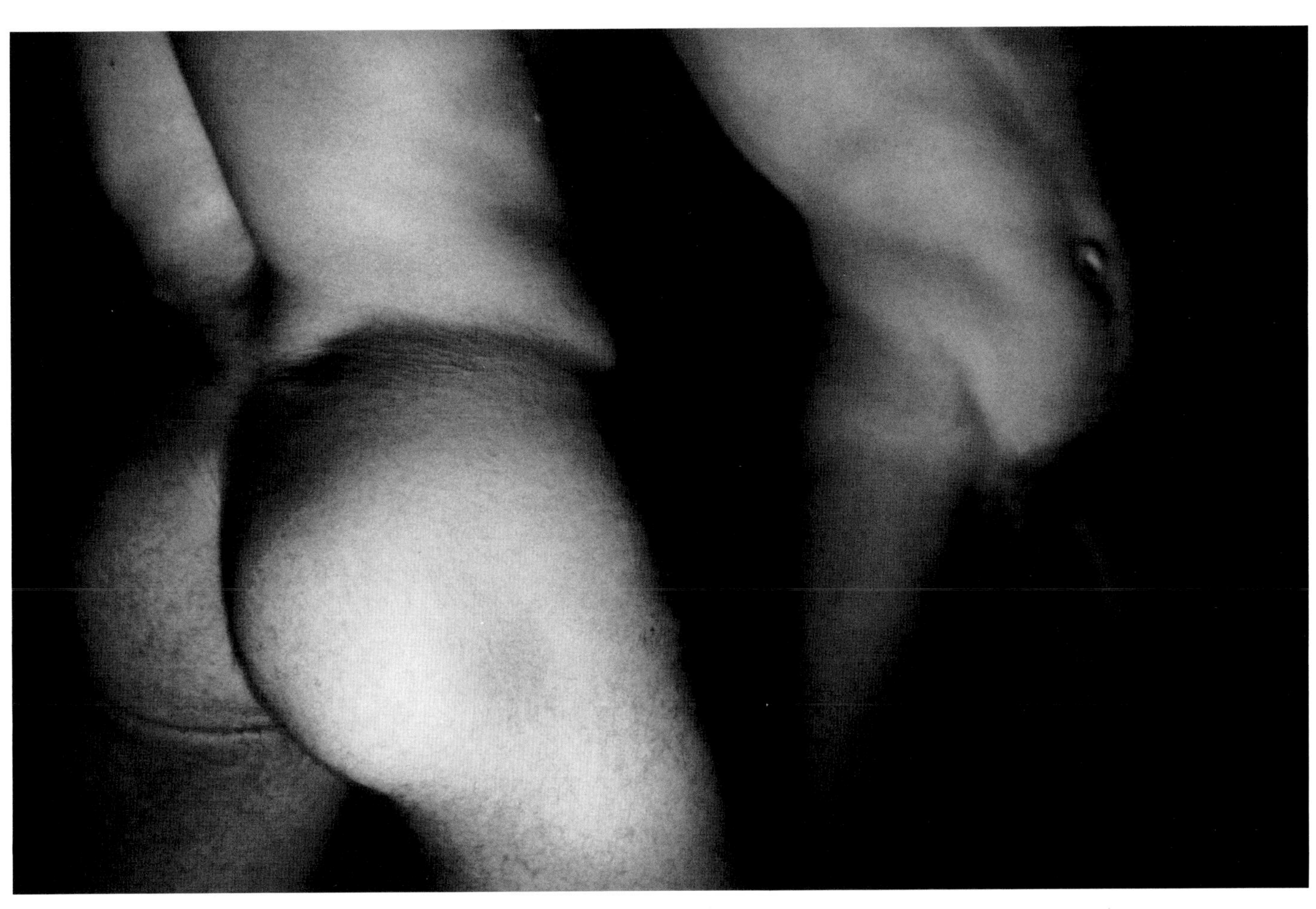

Amici del distretto, 1984

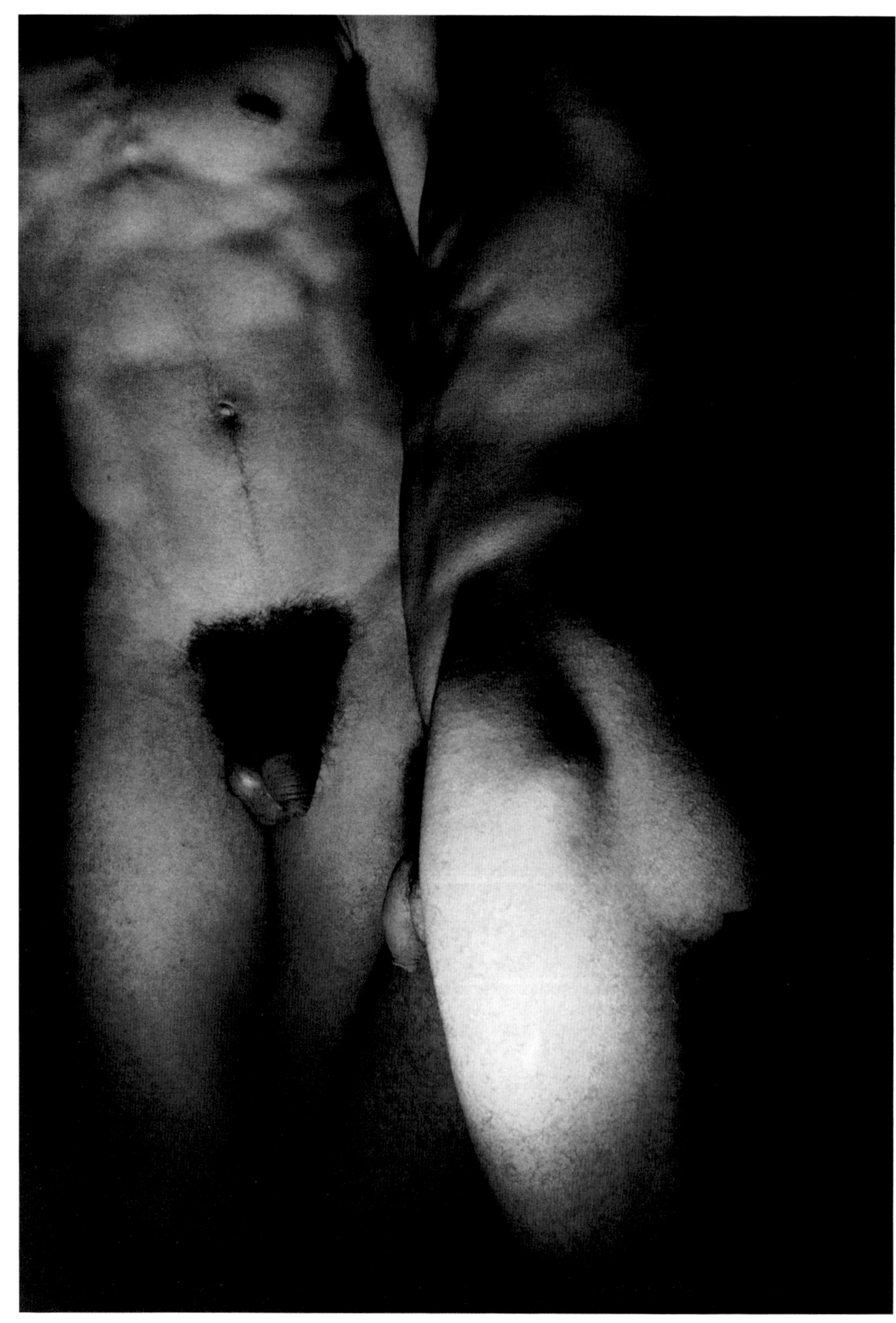

Gli Fratelli Romolo e Claudio, 1984

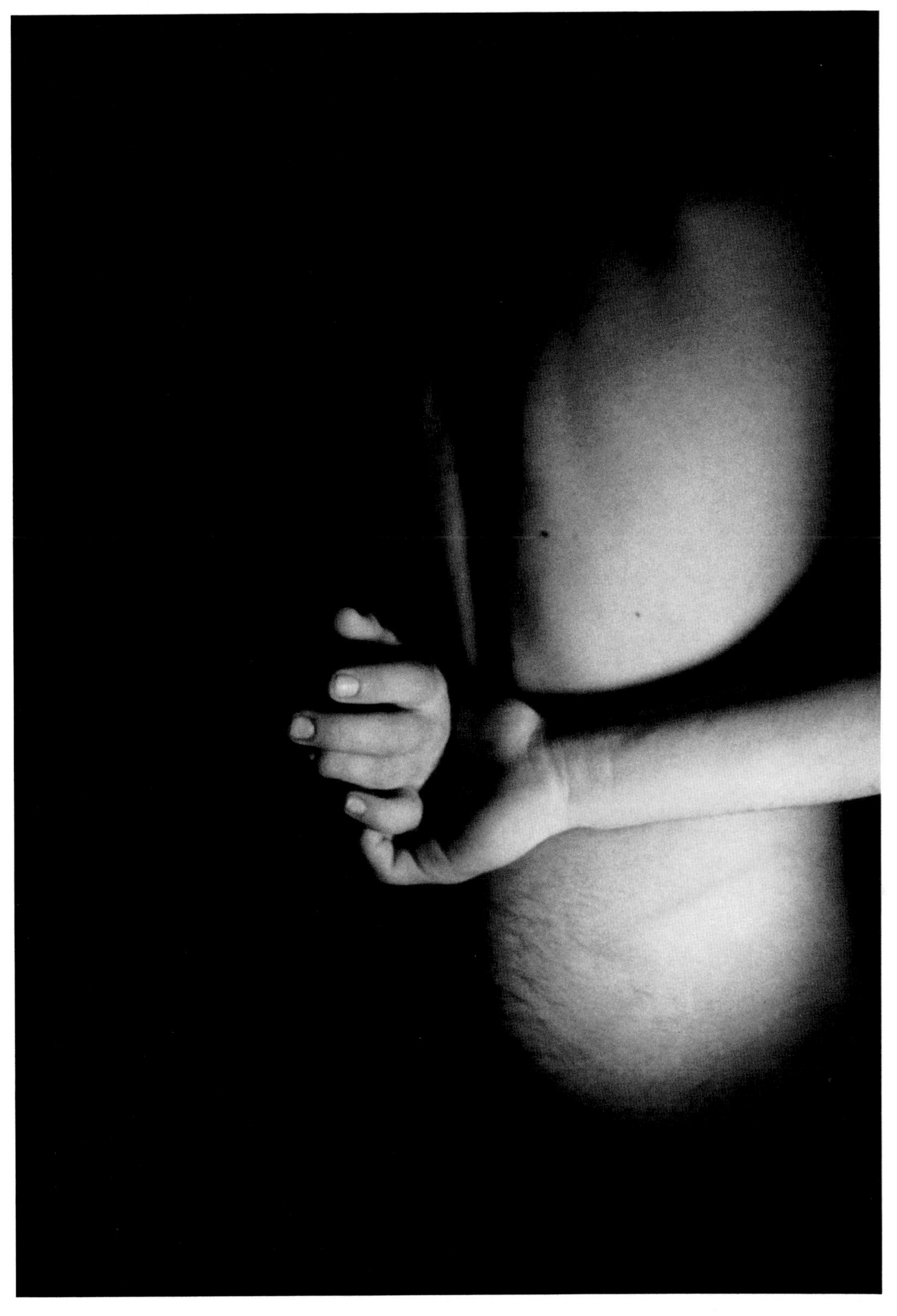

Bruno, 1984

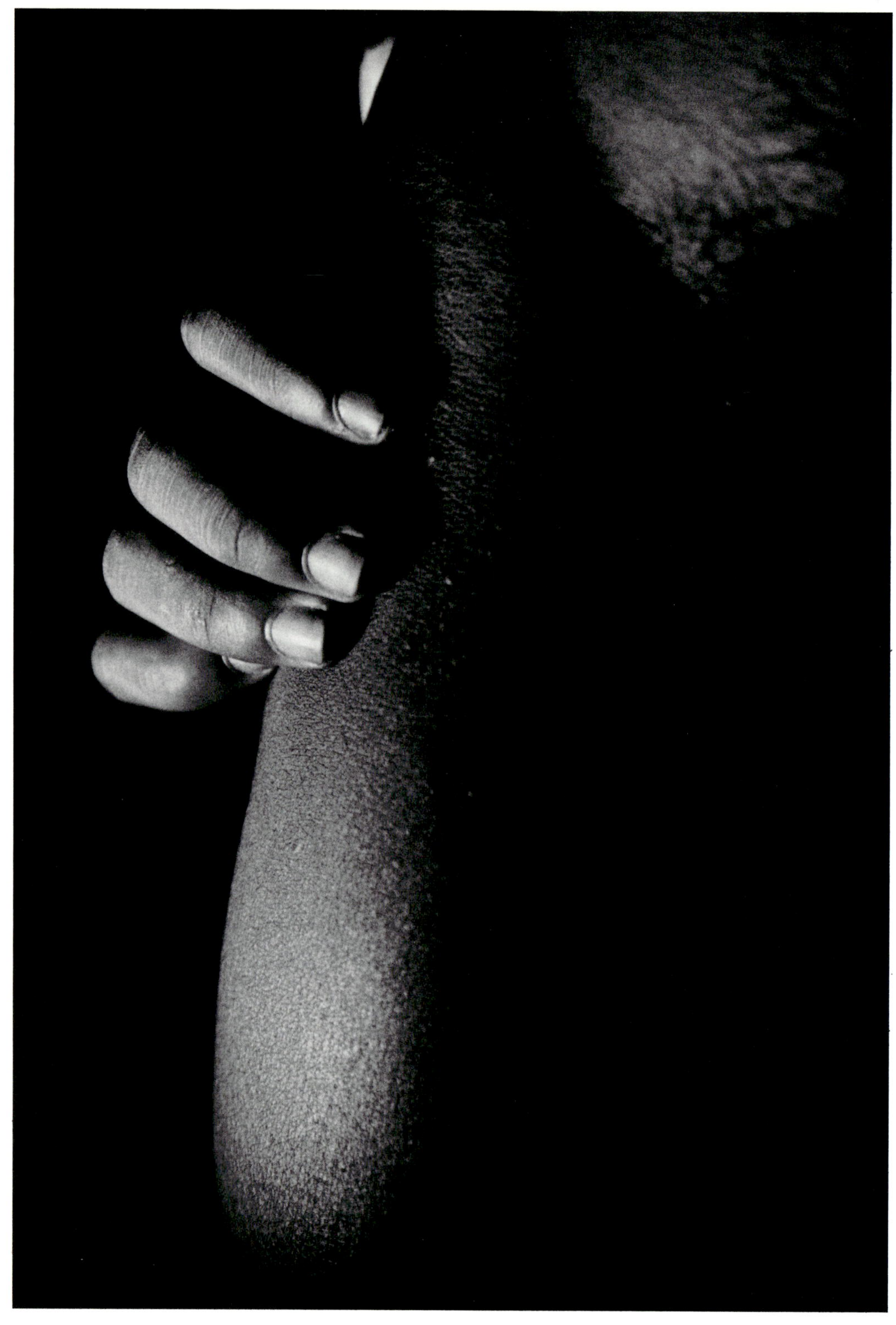

Ali, 1982

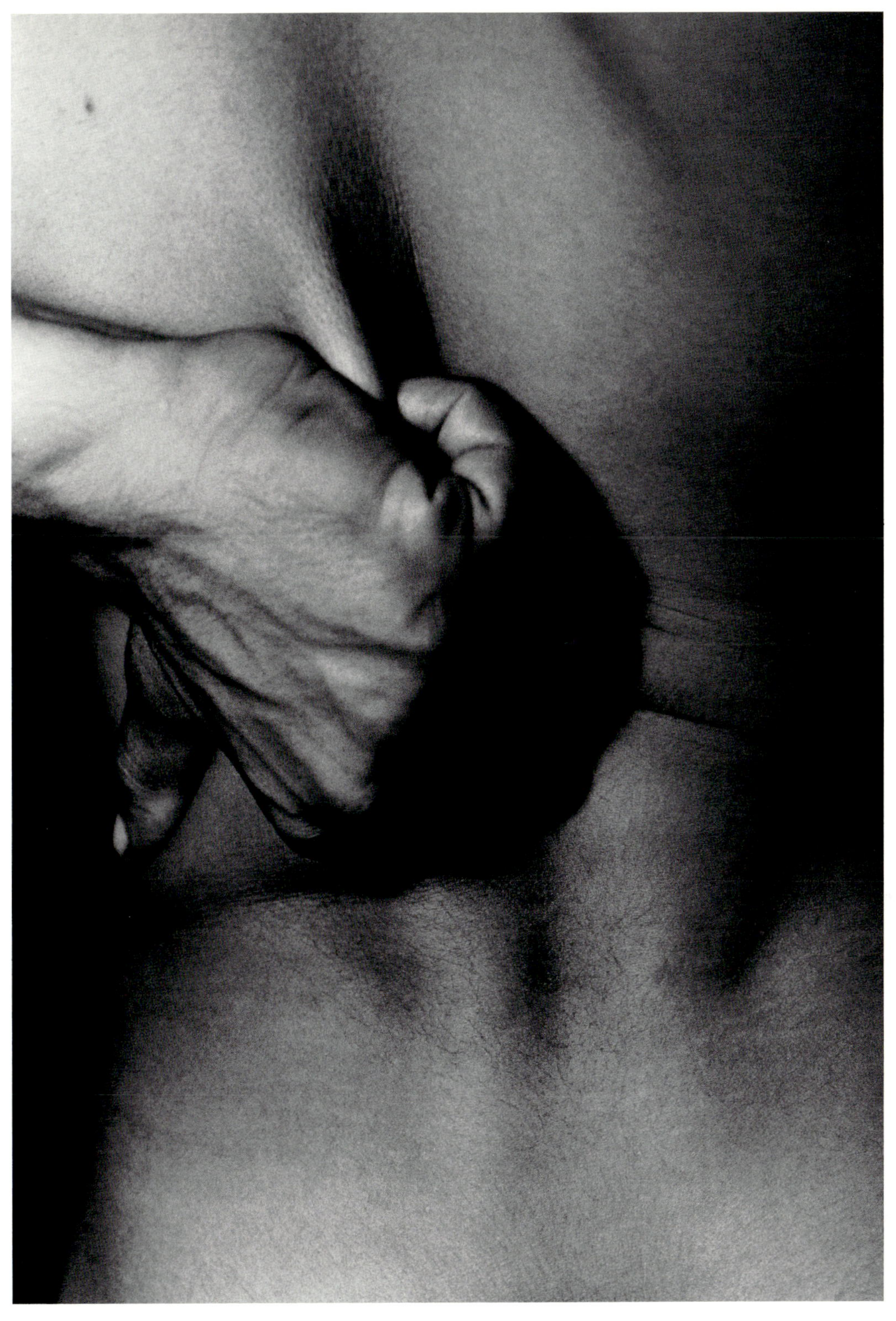

Albino, 1982

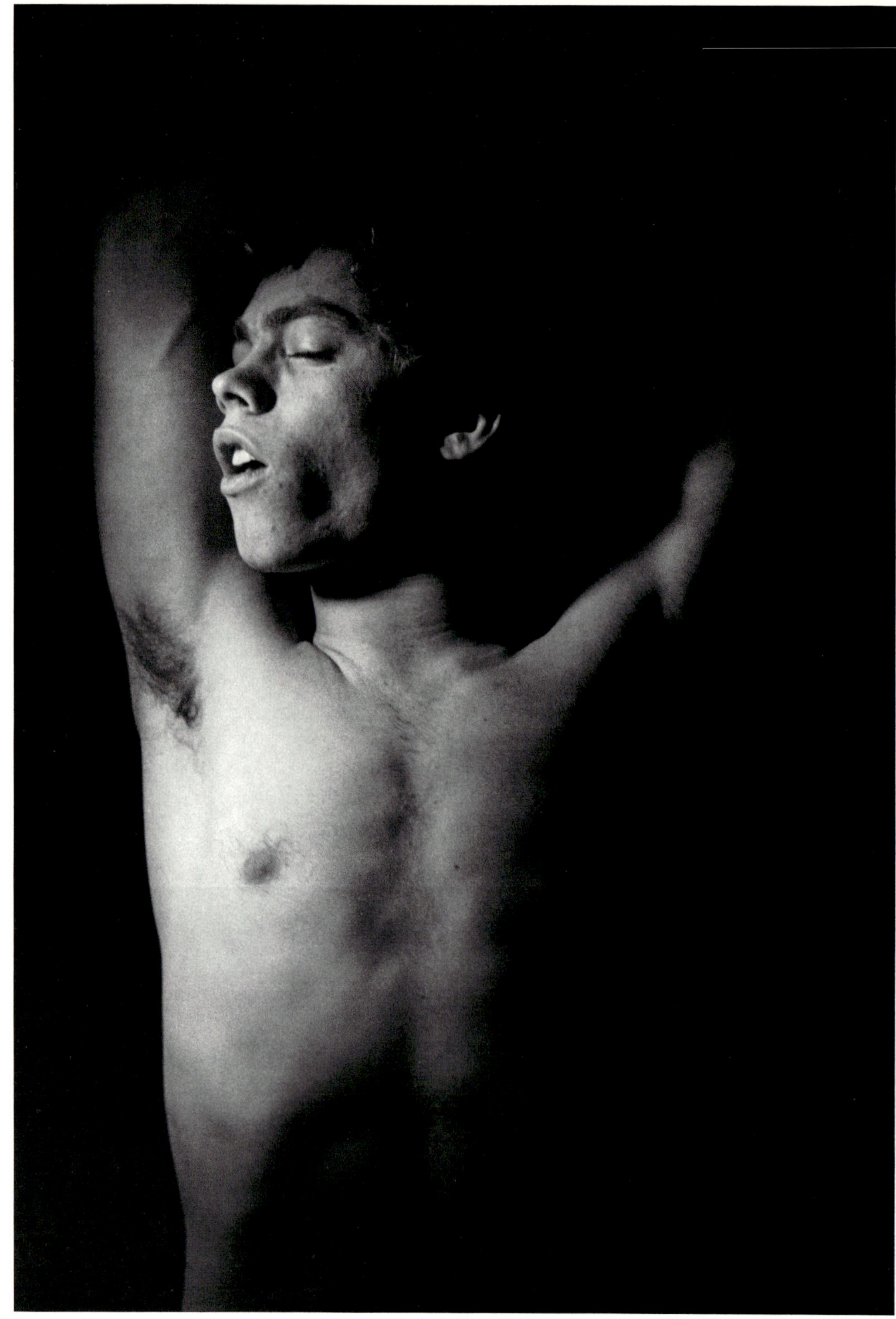

Bruno, 1984

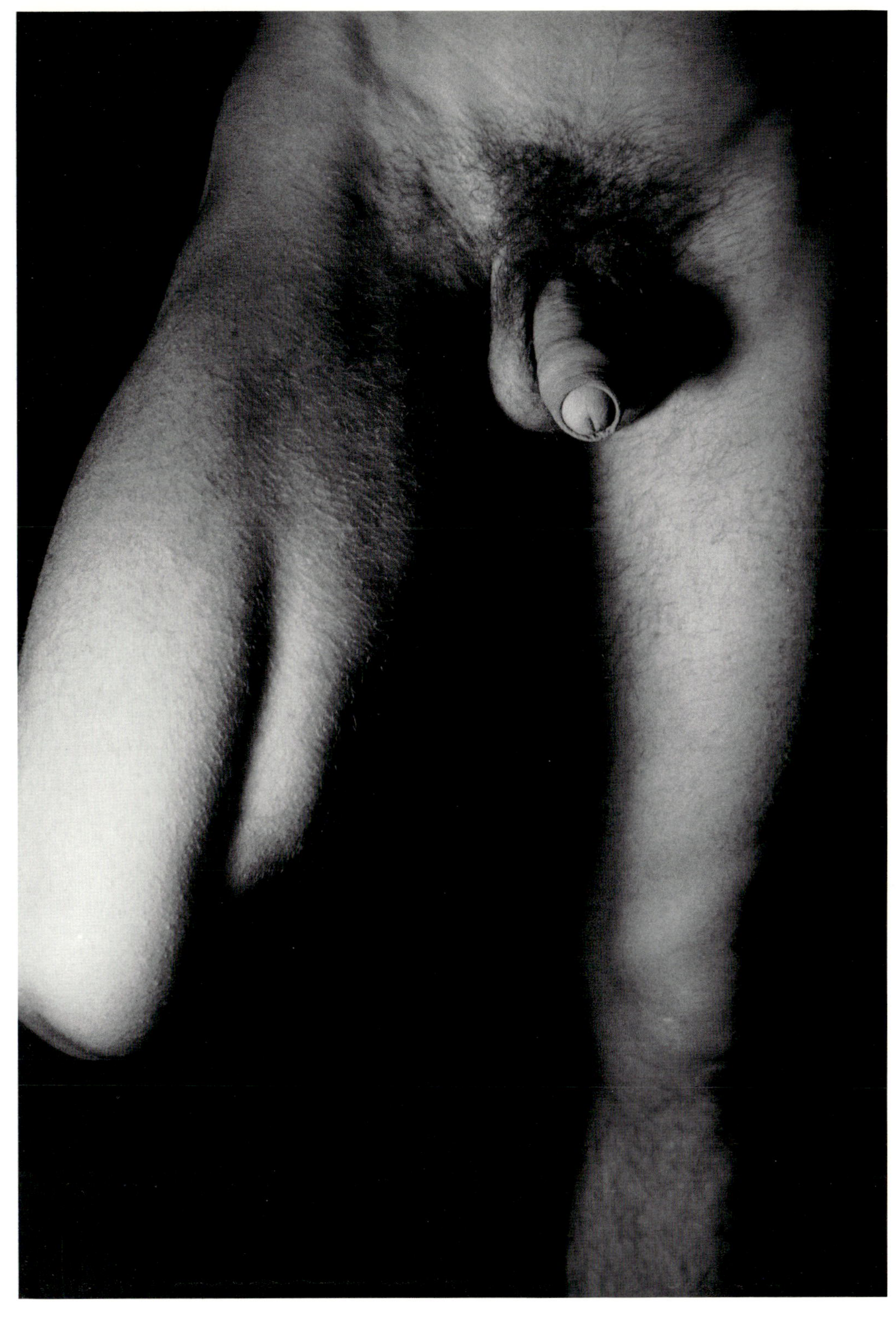

Carmine, 1984

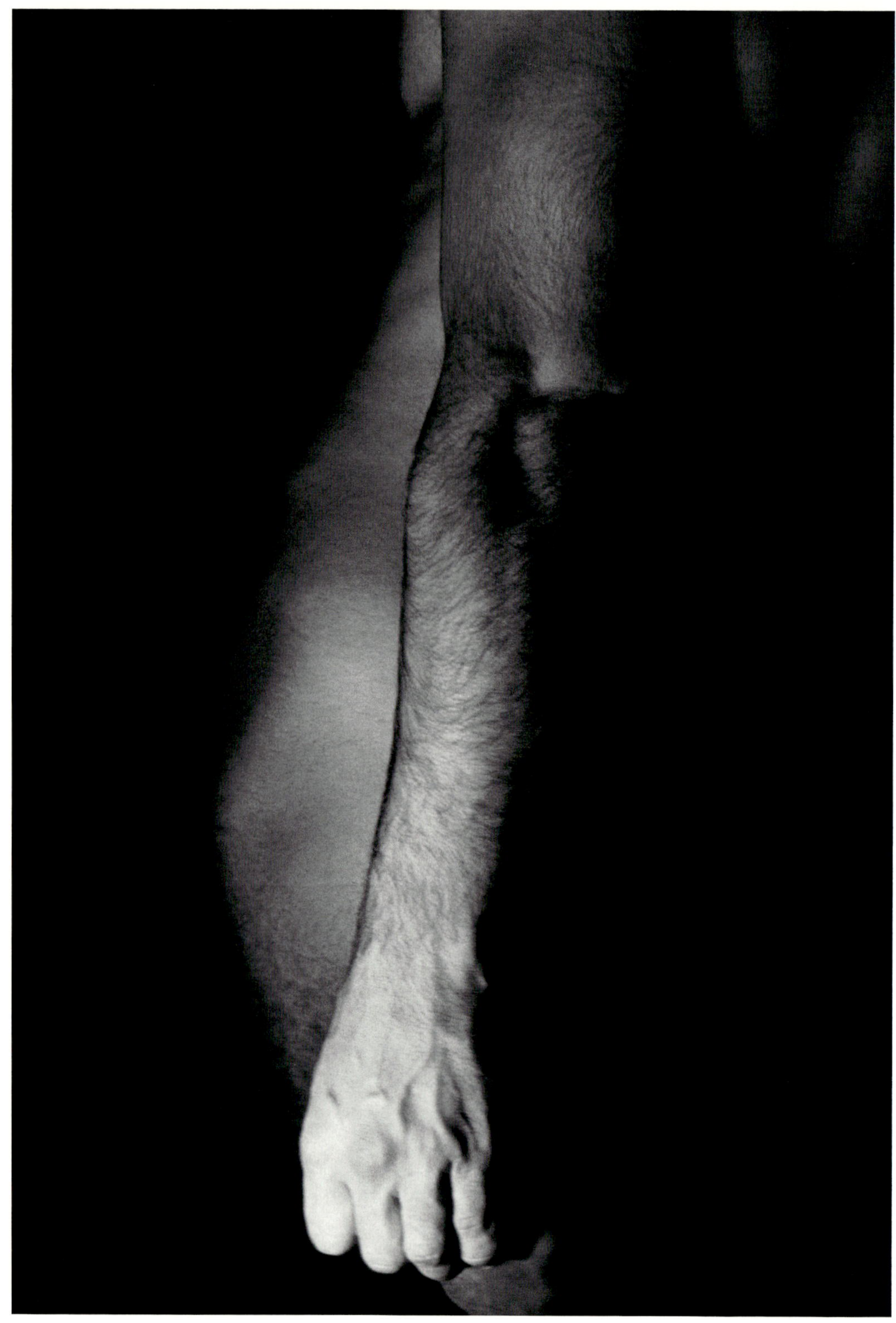

Nuccio, 1984

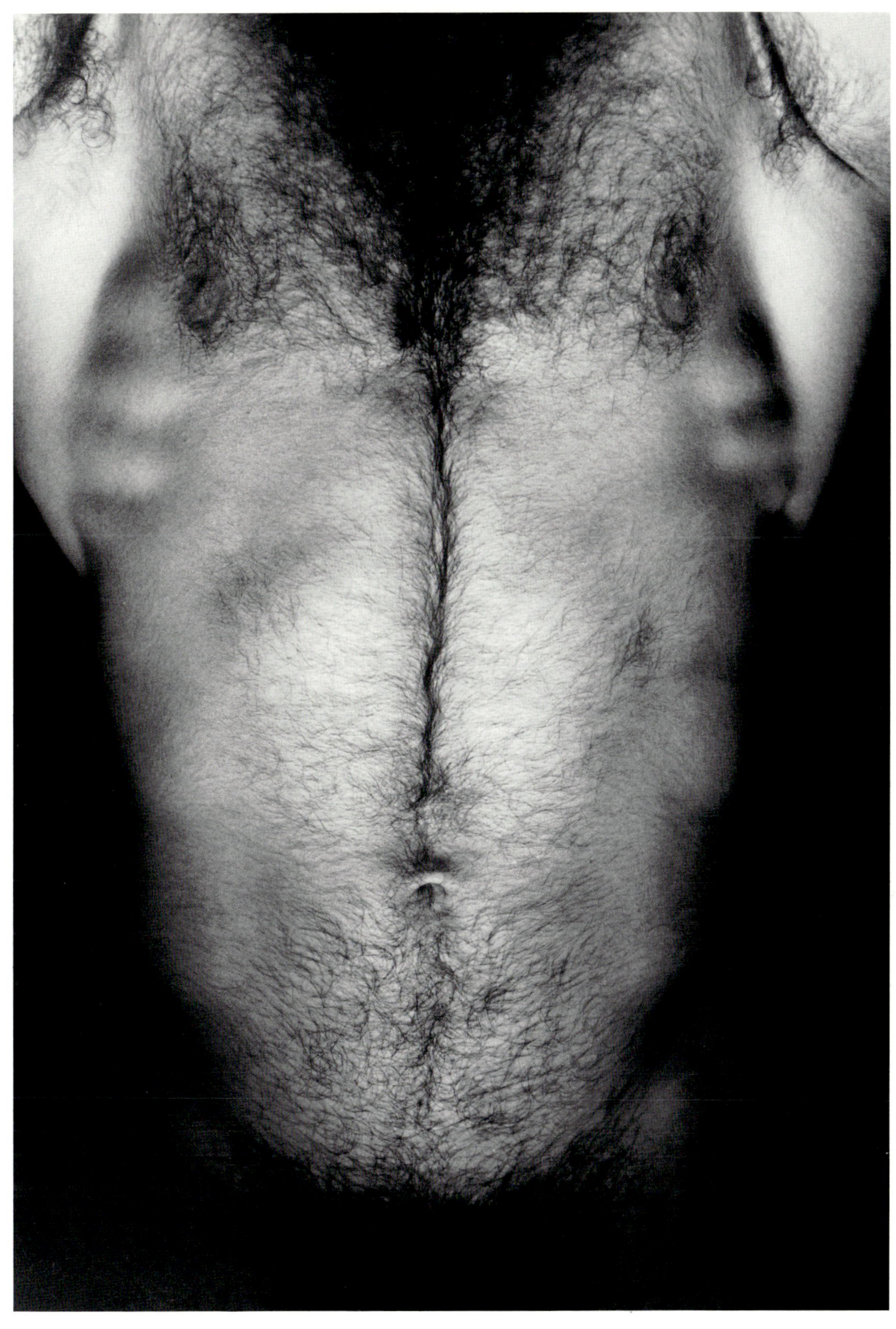

Nuccio, 1984

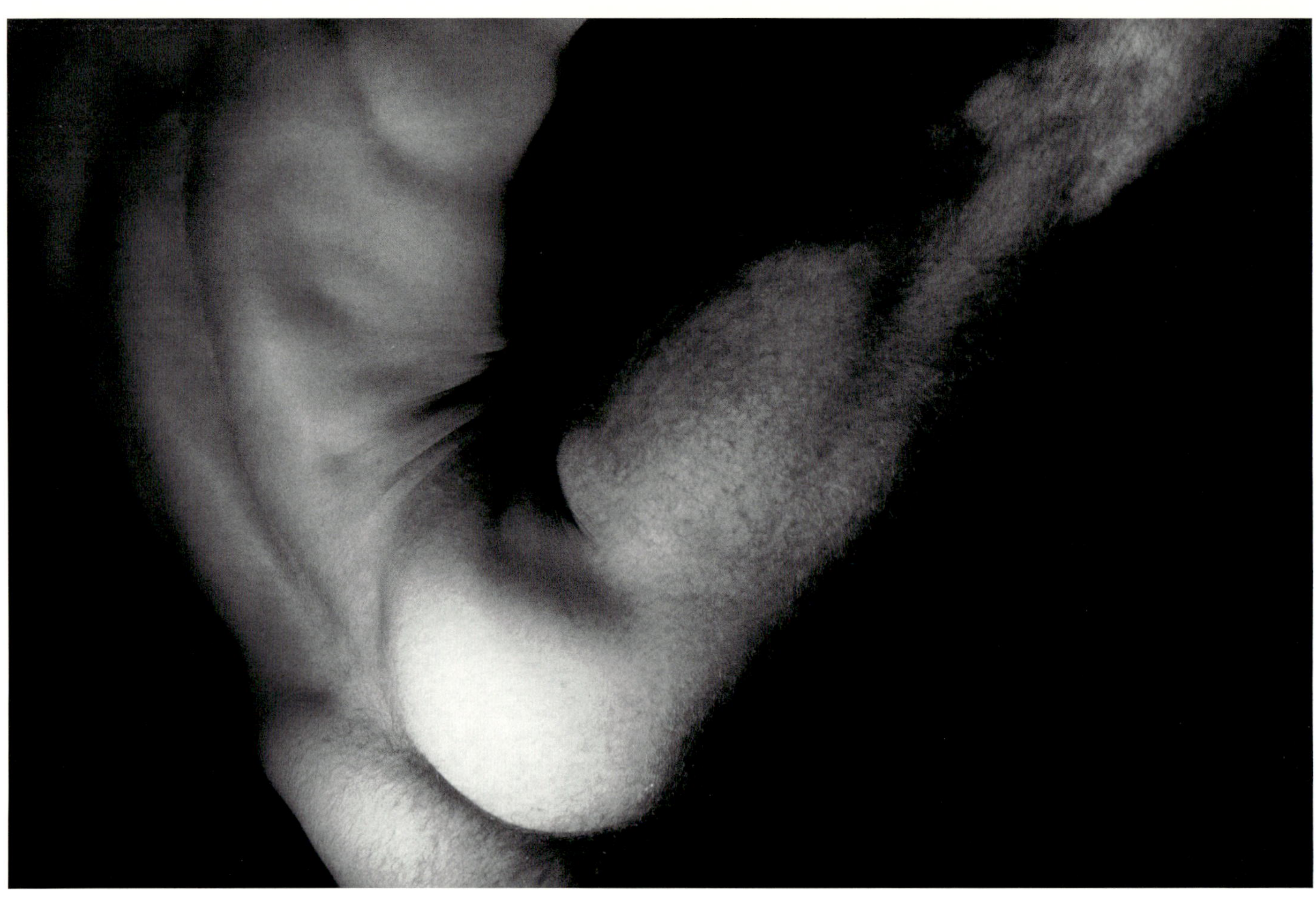

 Nuccio, 1984

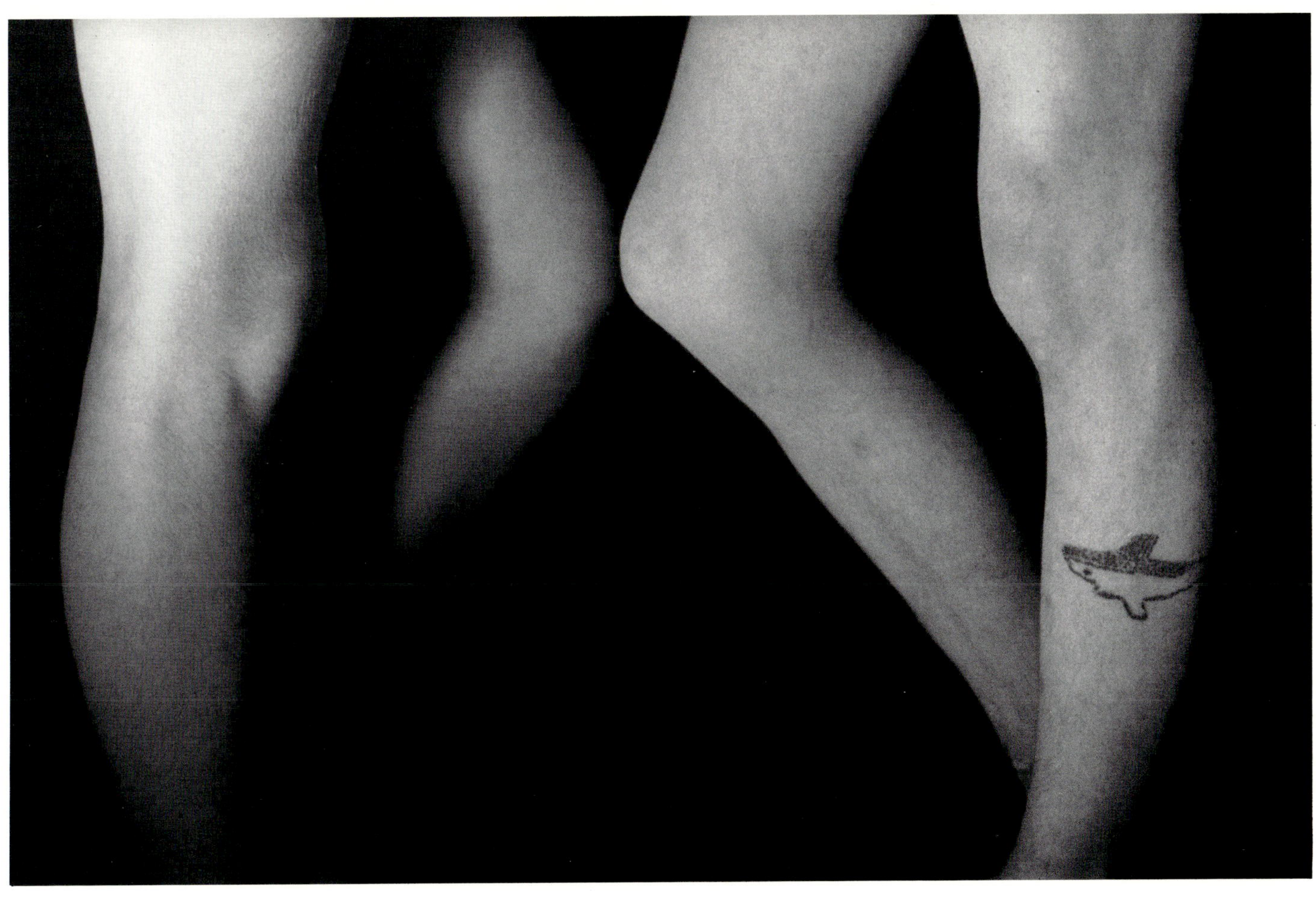

Filippo ed Antonio, 1983

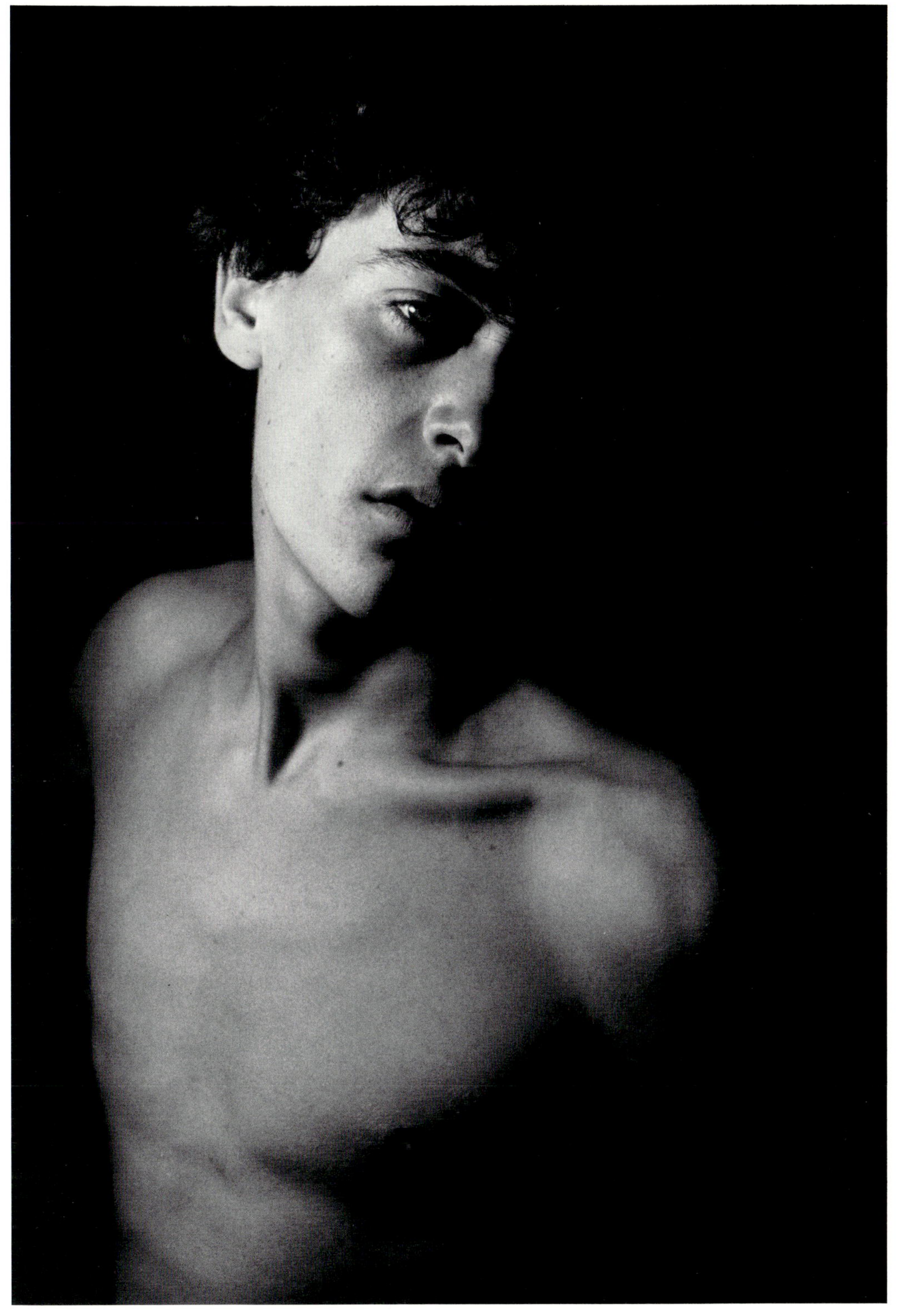

Fabio, 1985

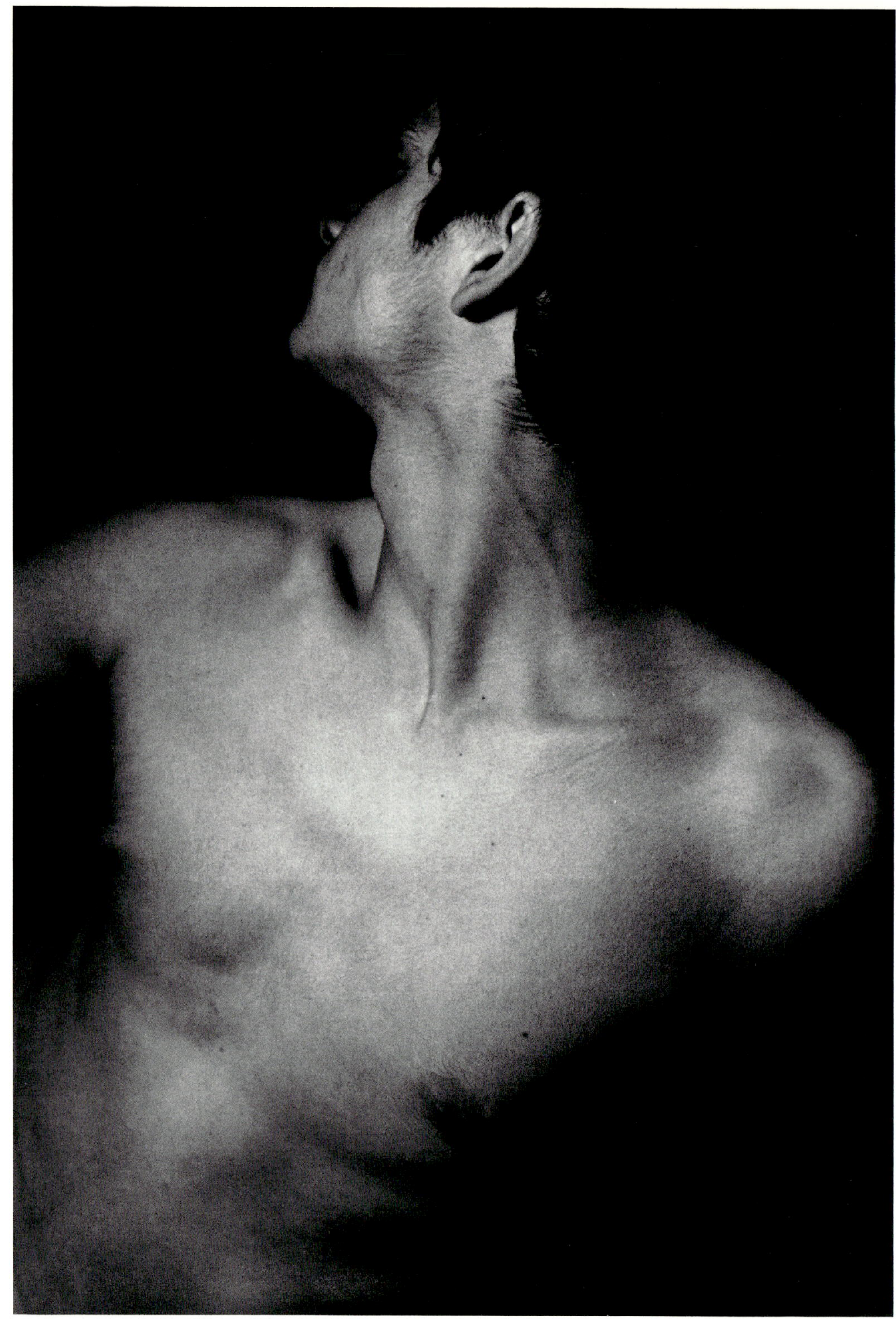

Gennaro, 1984

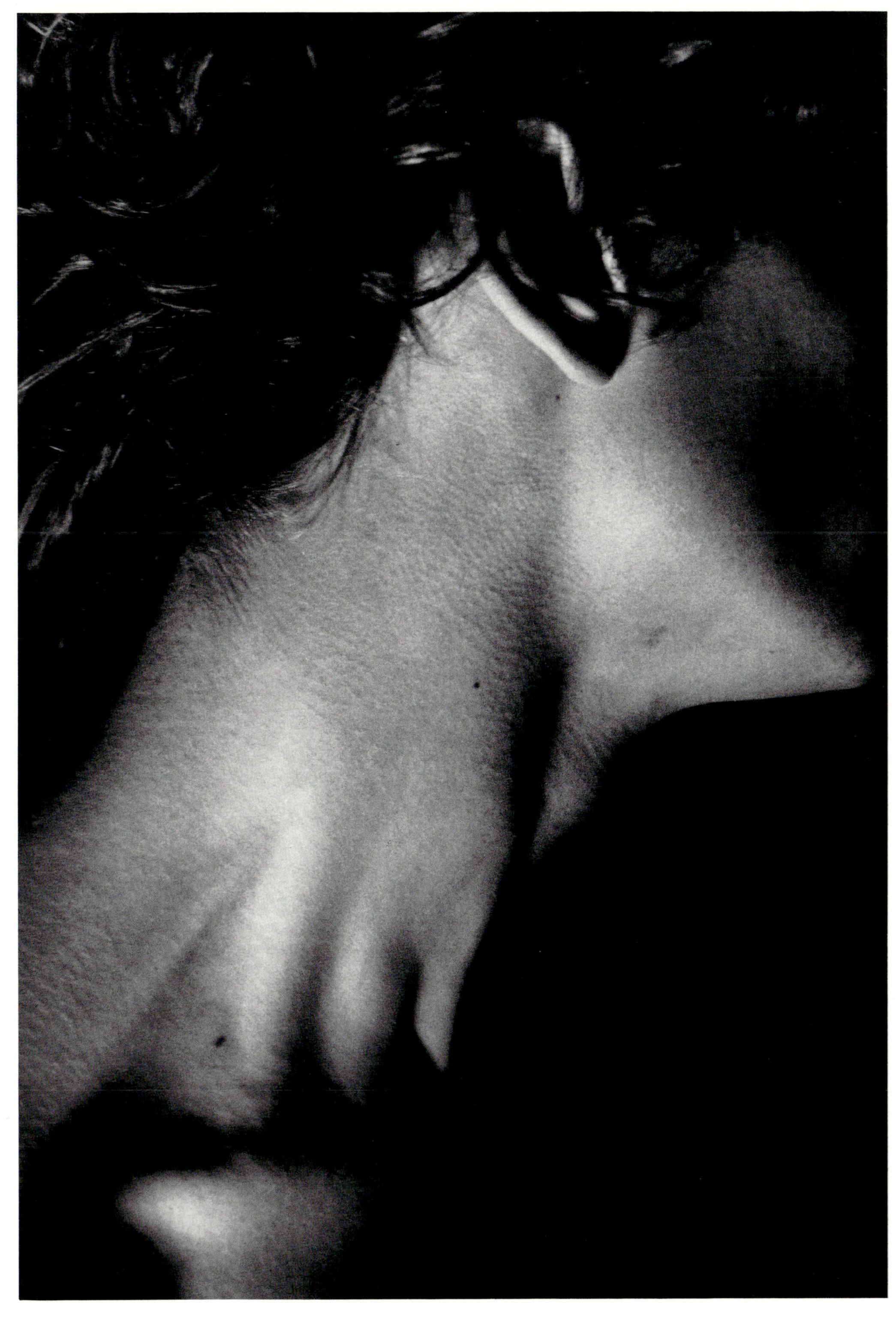

Edoardo, 1984

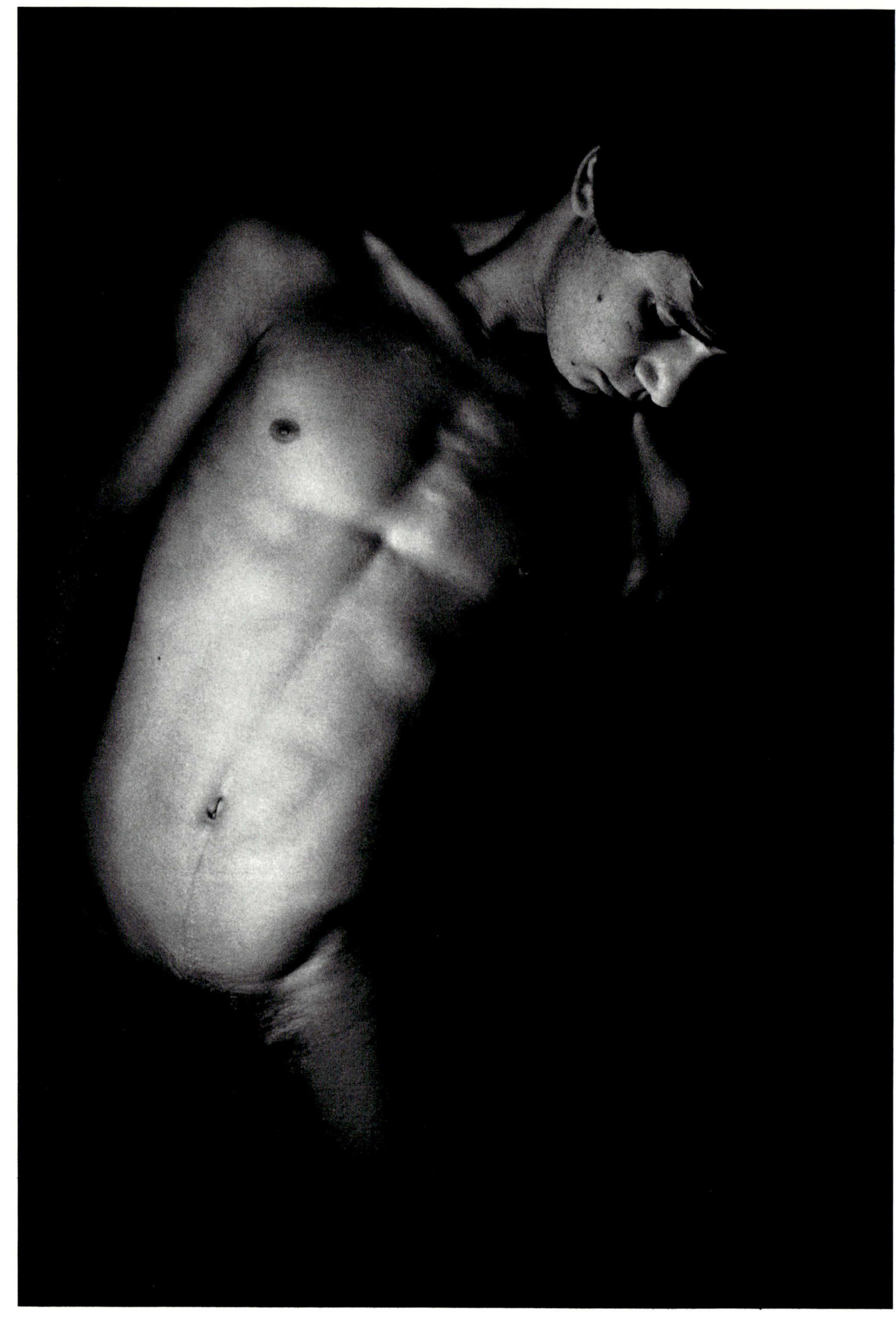

Carmine, 1984

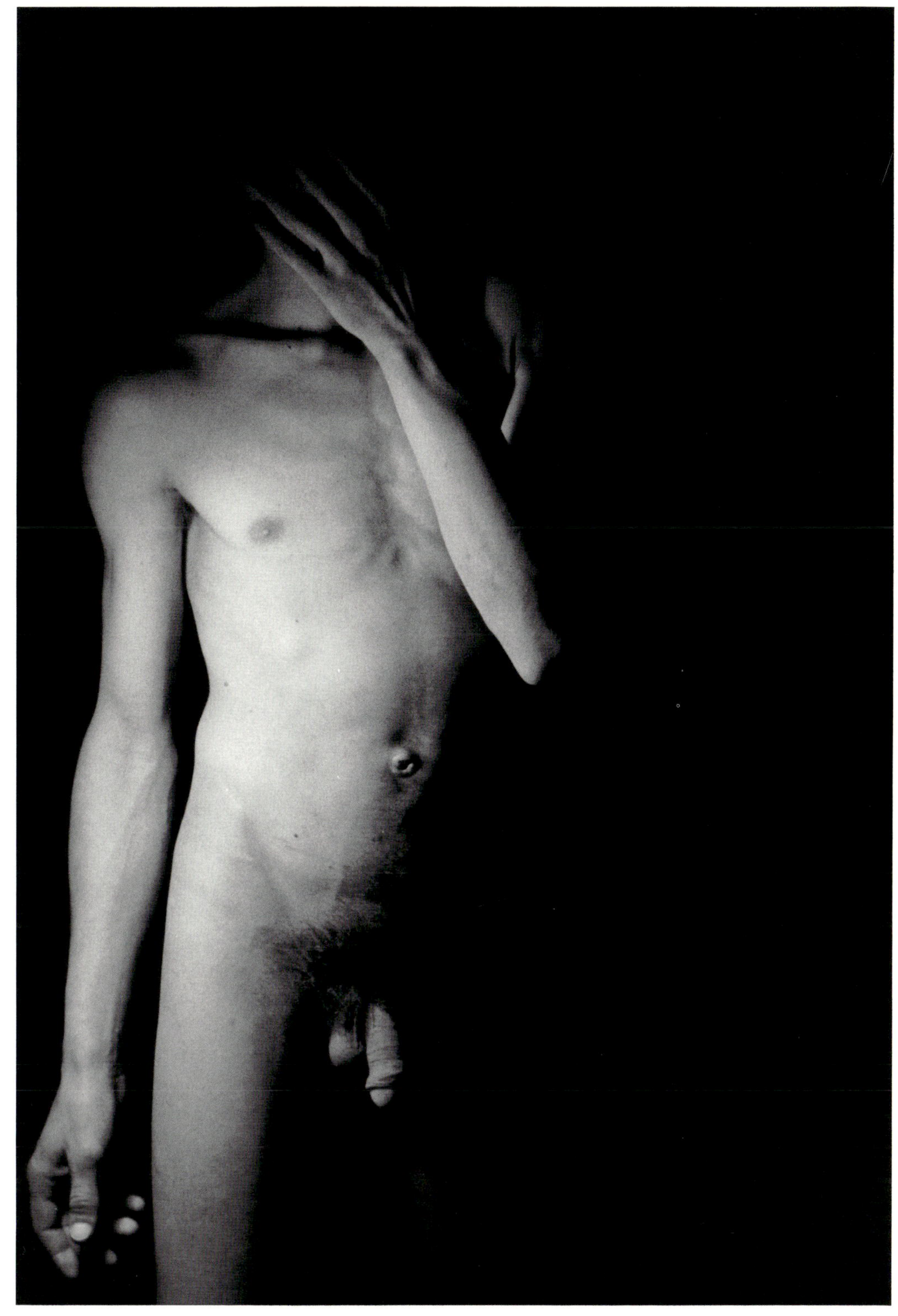

Franchino, 1985

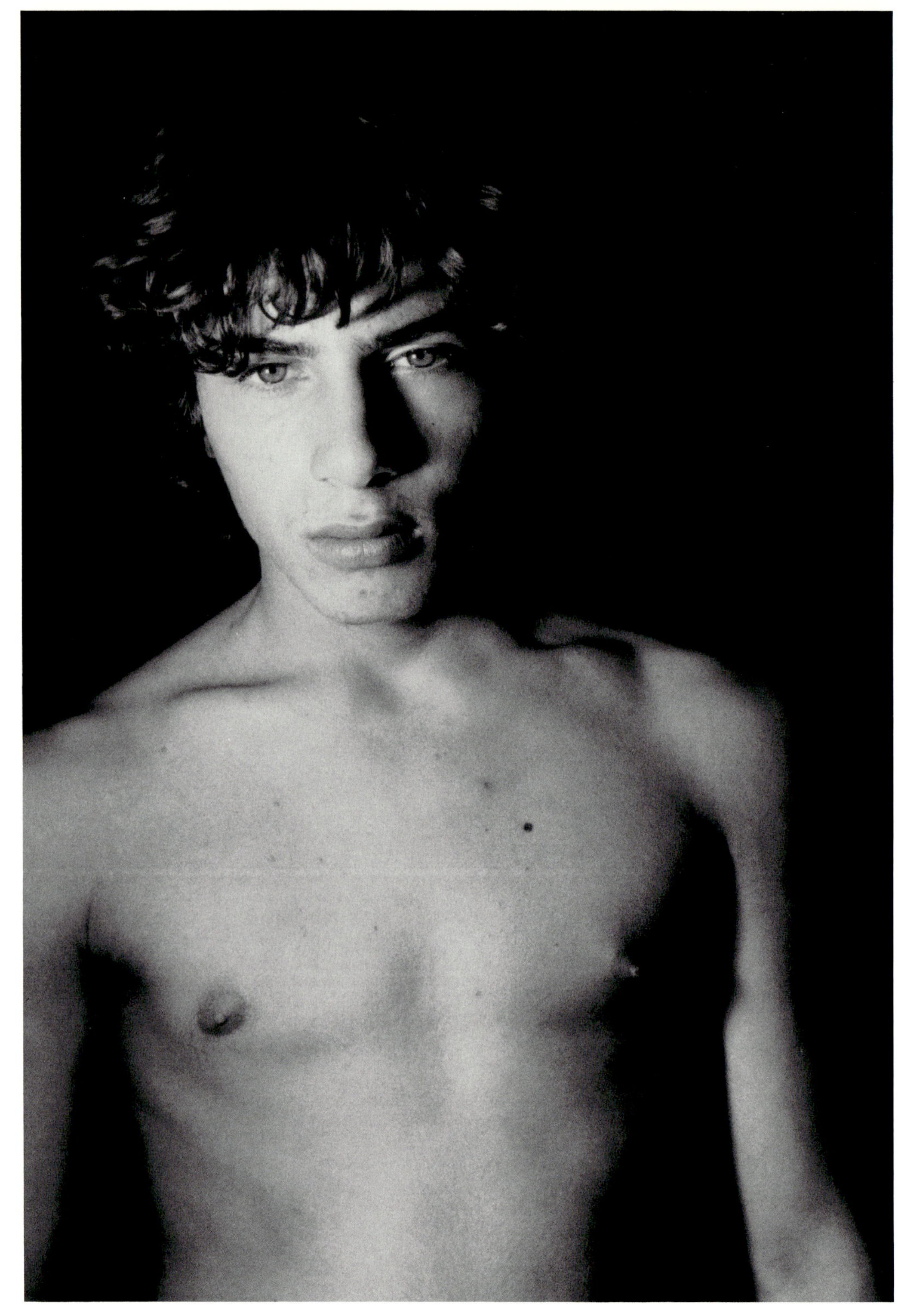

 Michele, 1985

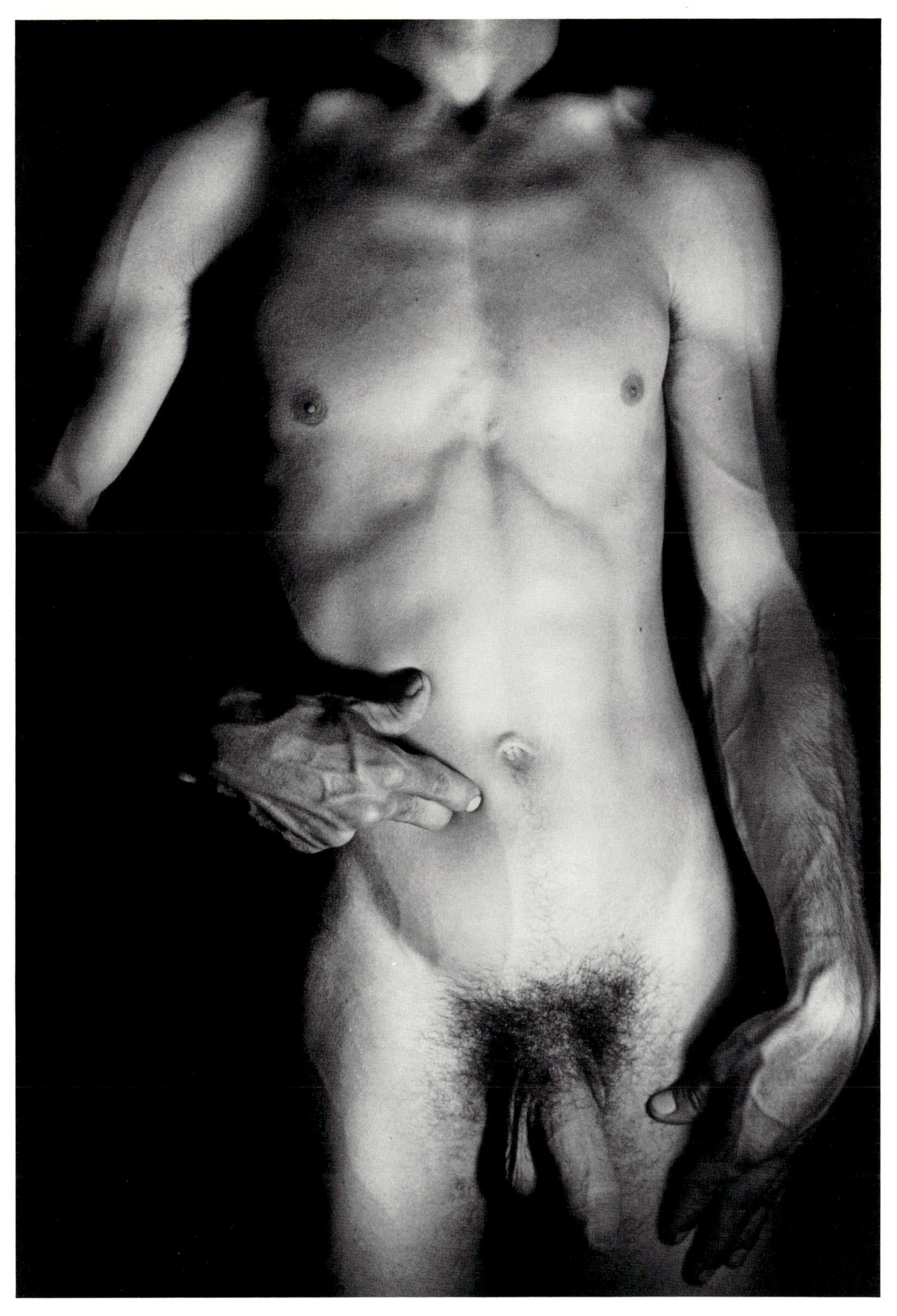

Andrea, 1985

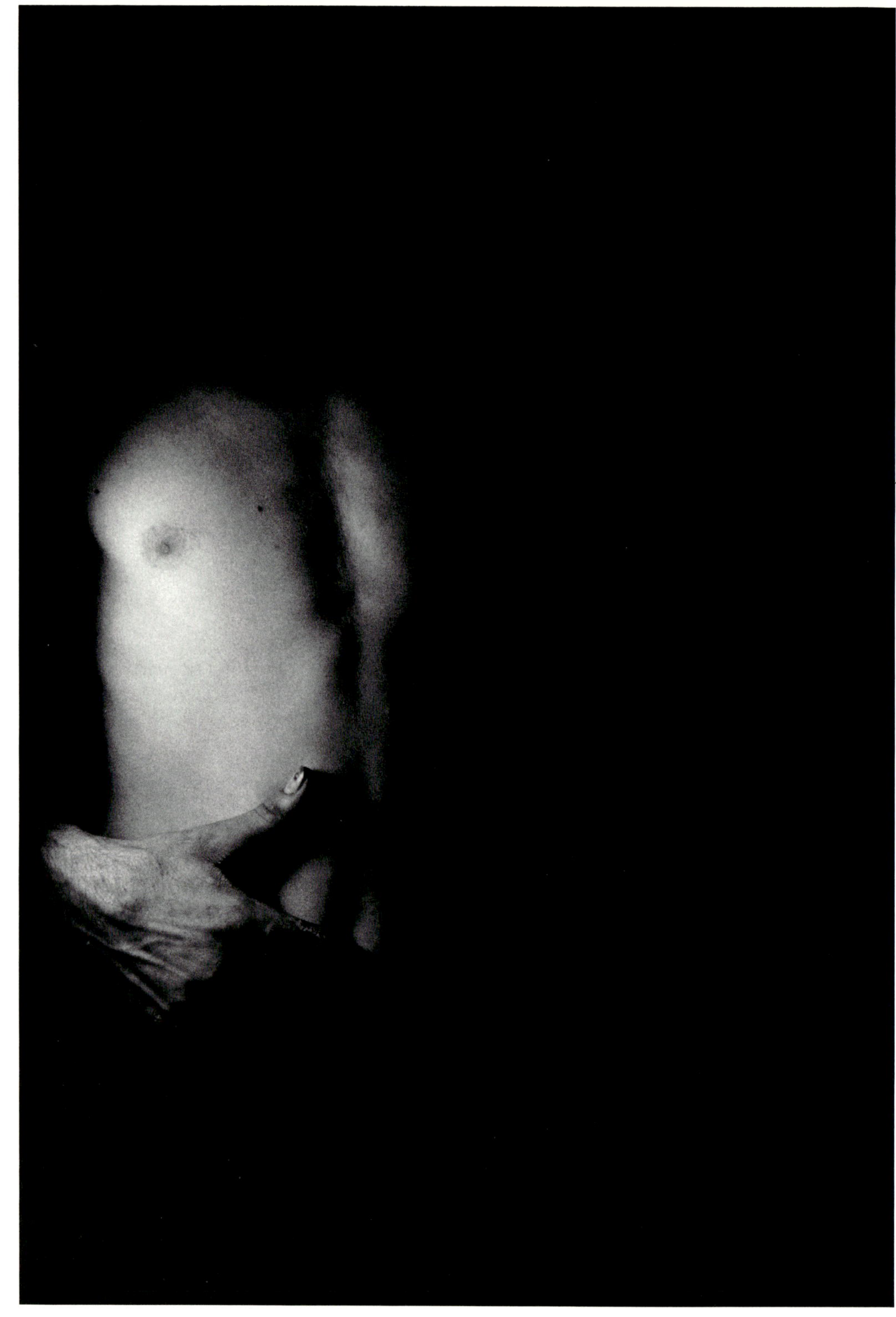

Gianni, 1985

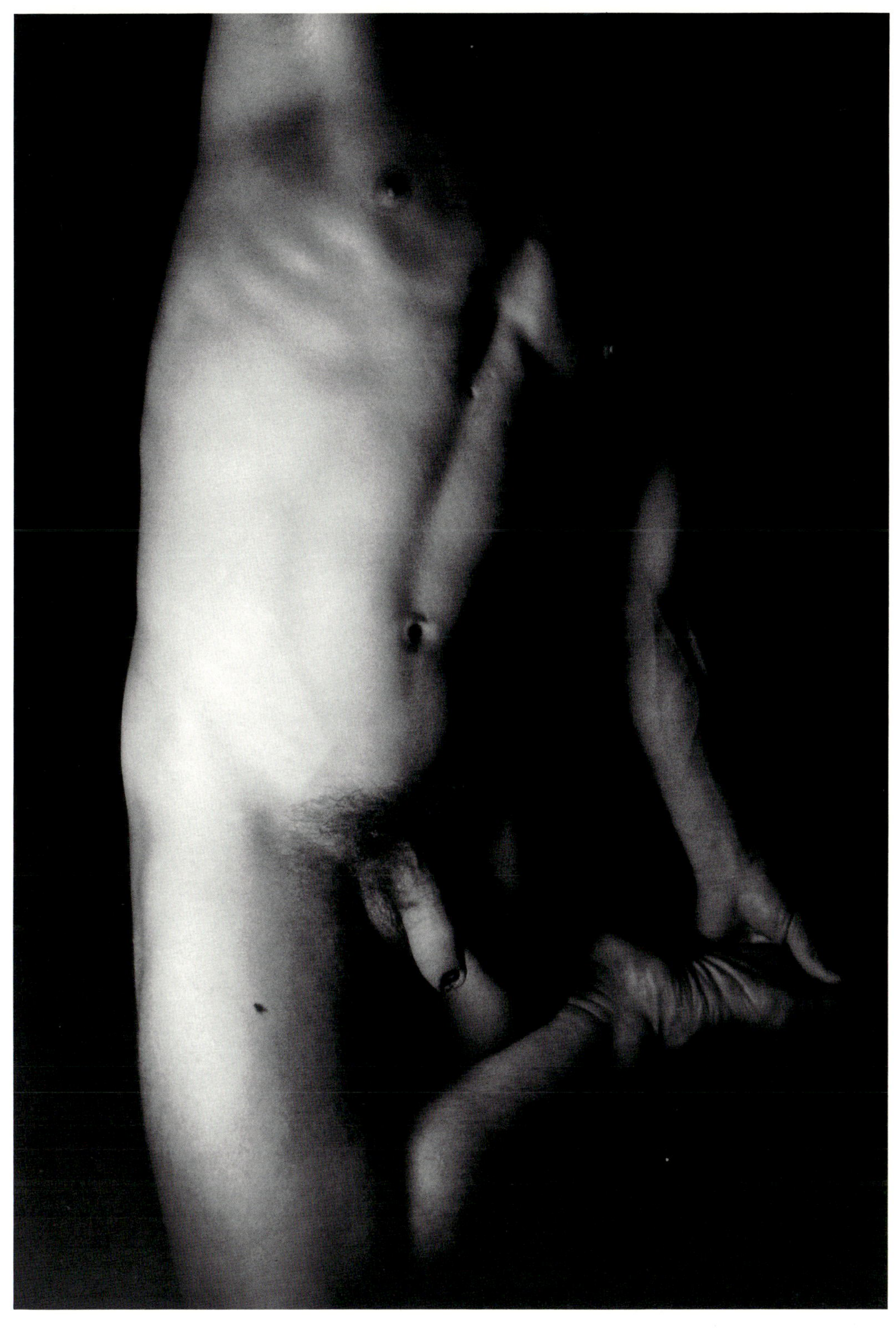

Sandro, 1985

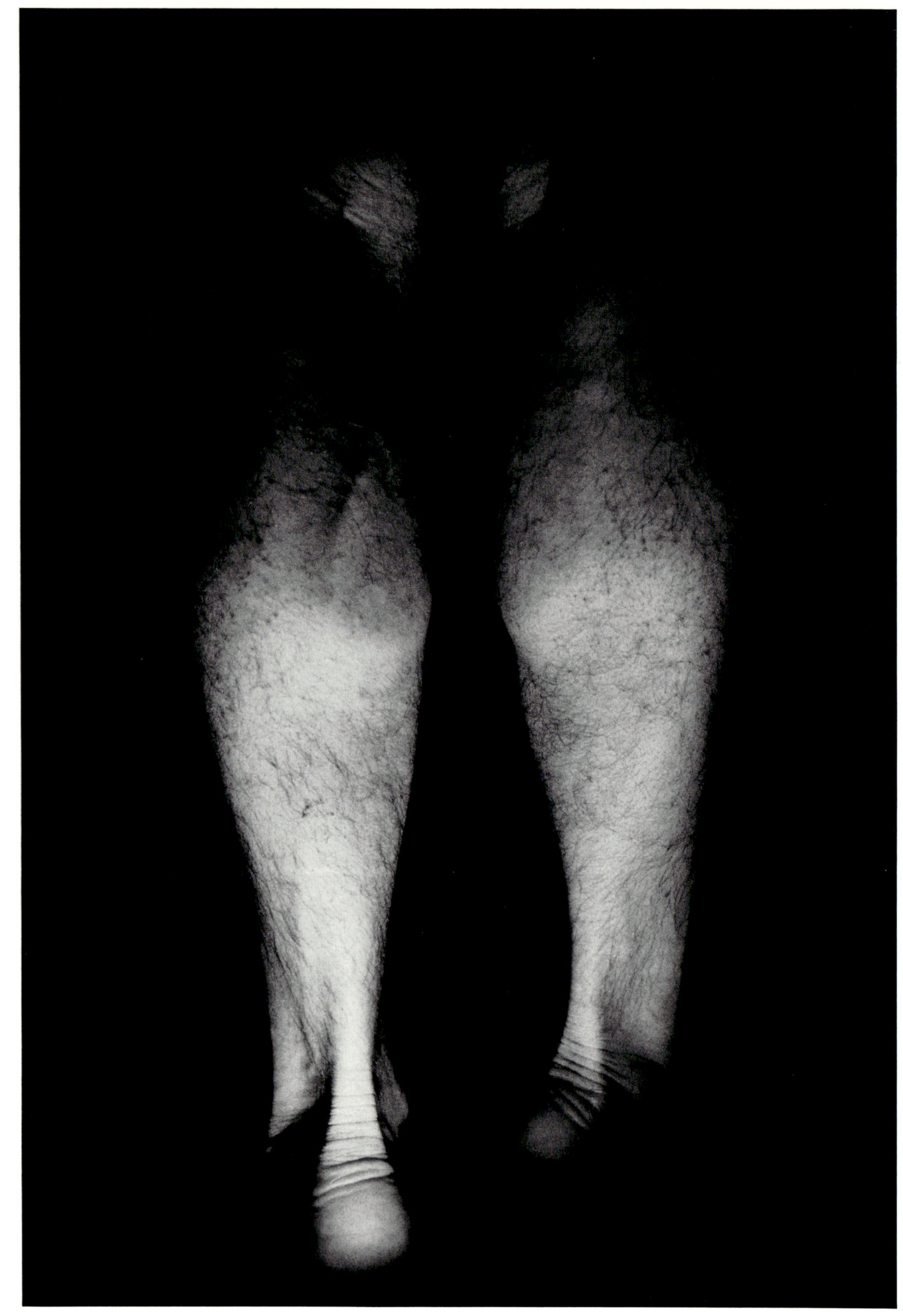

Ian, 1984

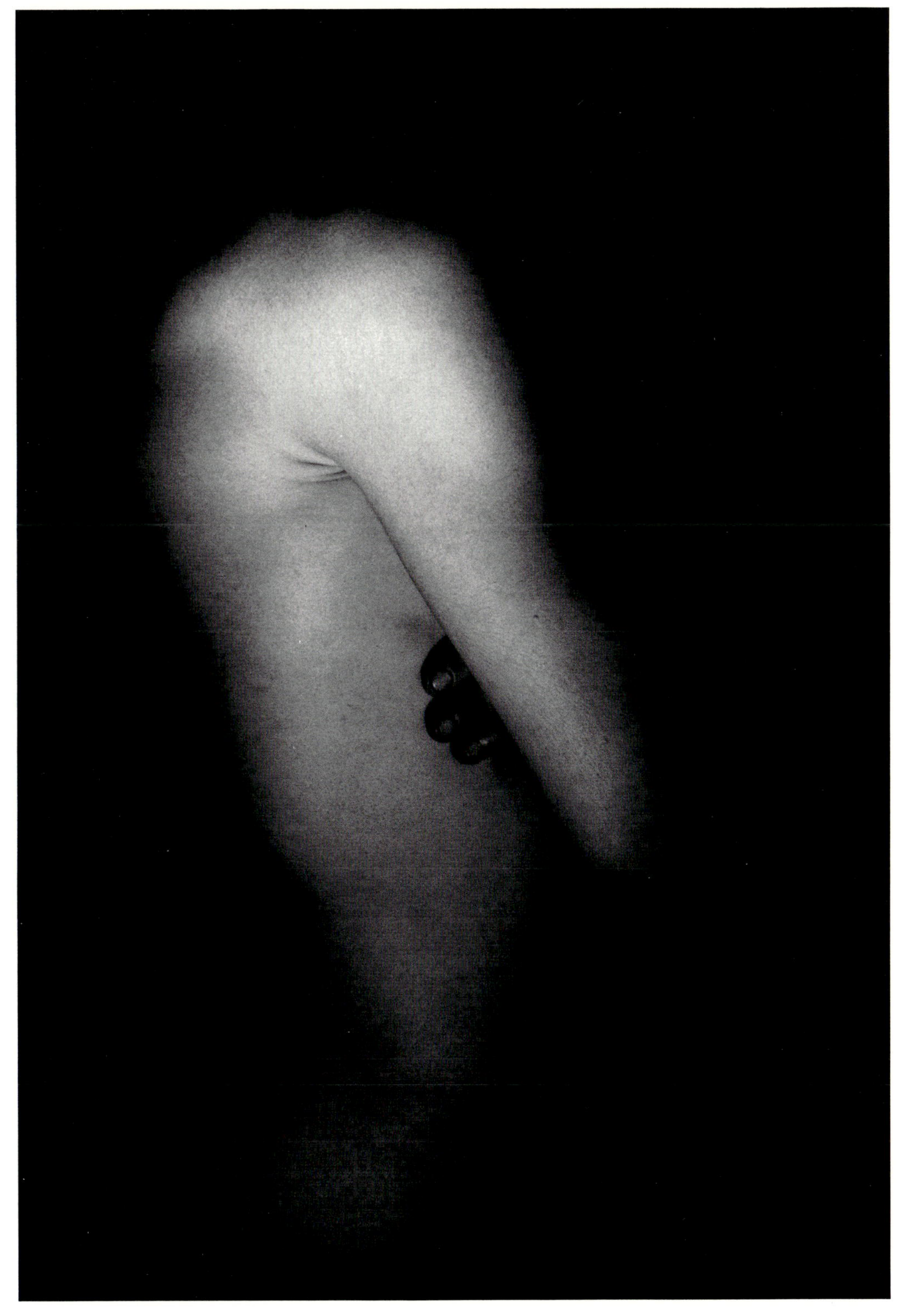

Gennaro, 1984

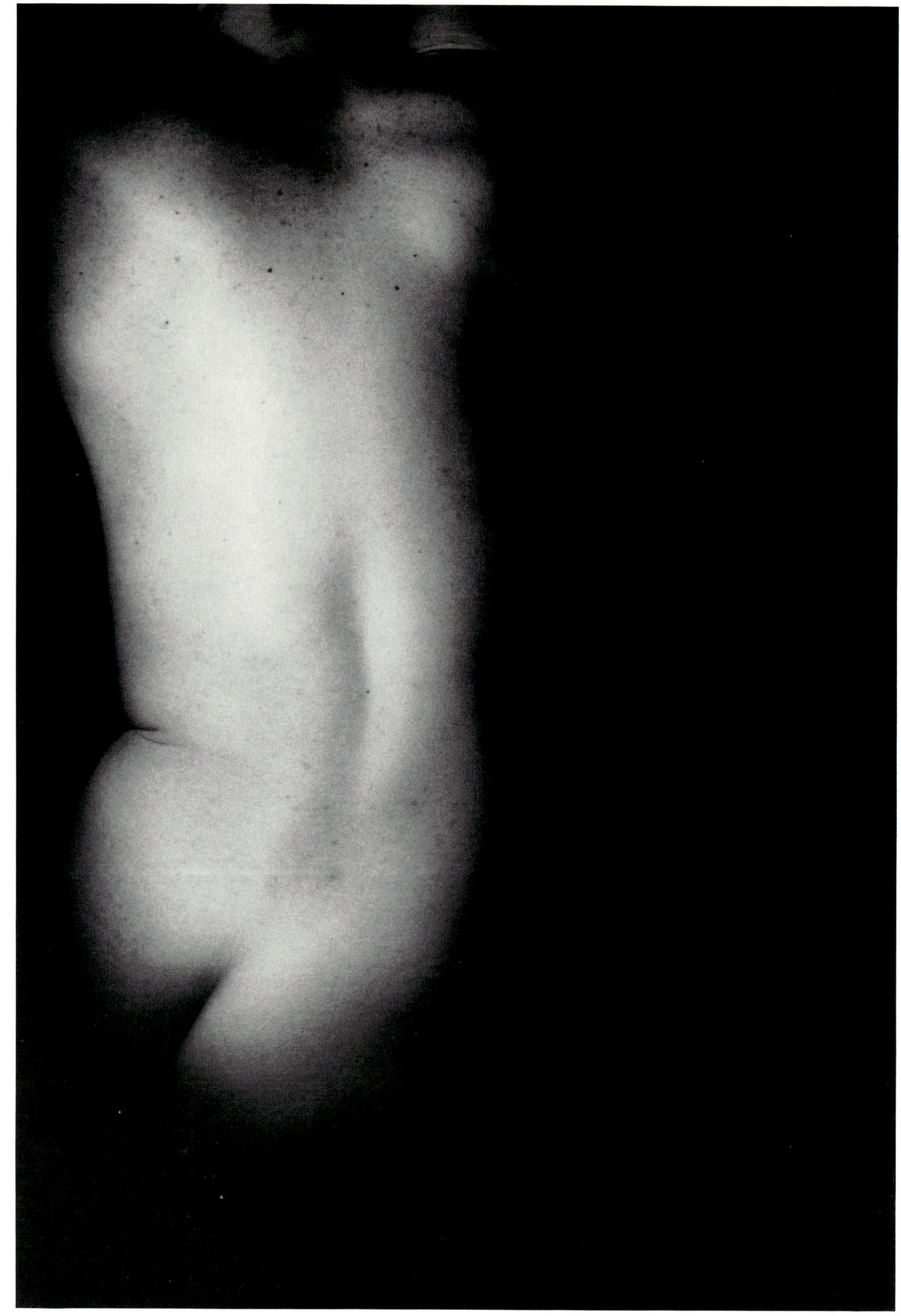

Ian, 1984

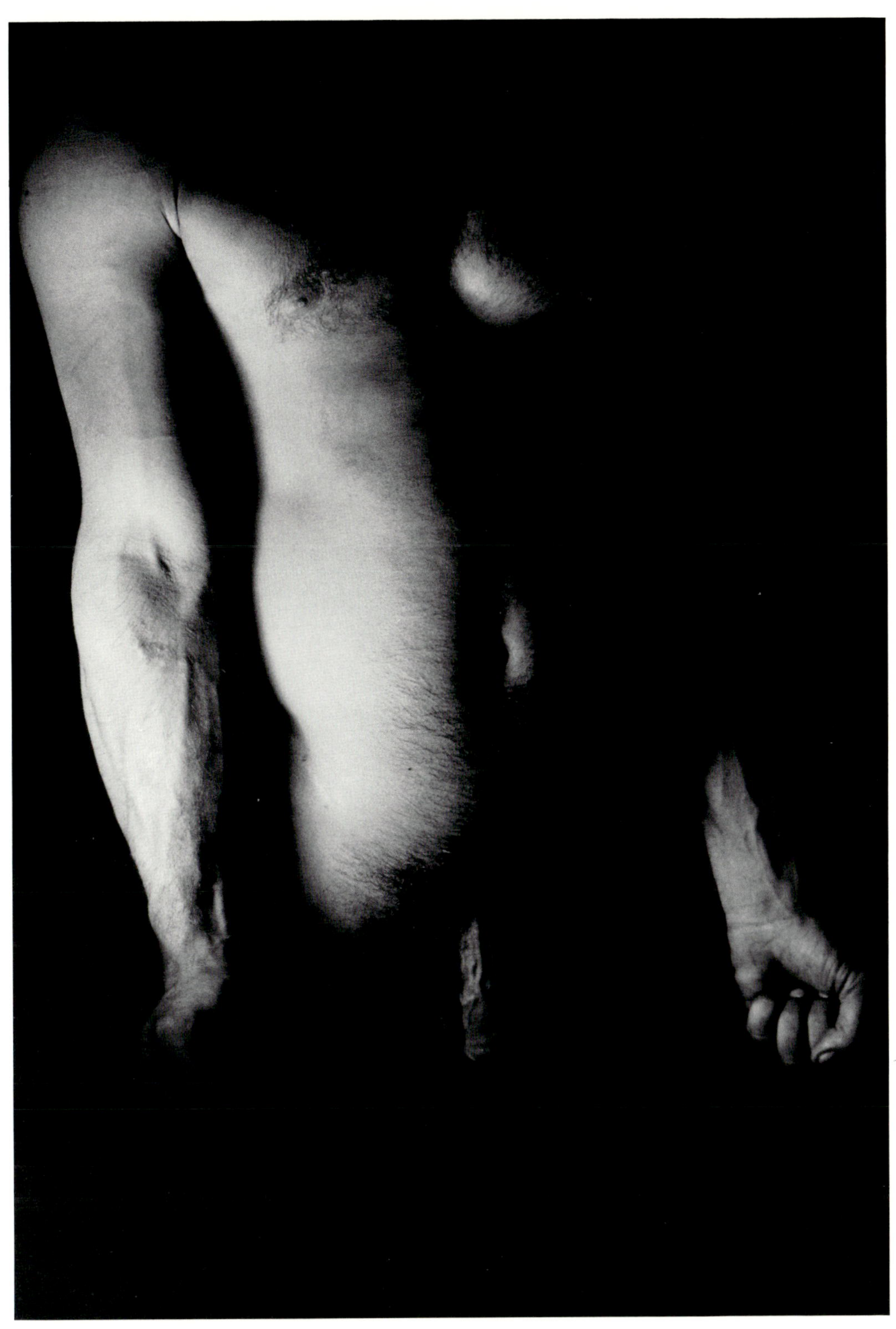

Il Zingaro (Omaggio a Pier Paolo Pasolini), 1984

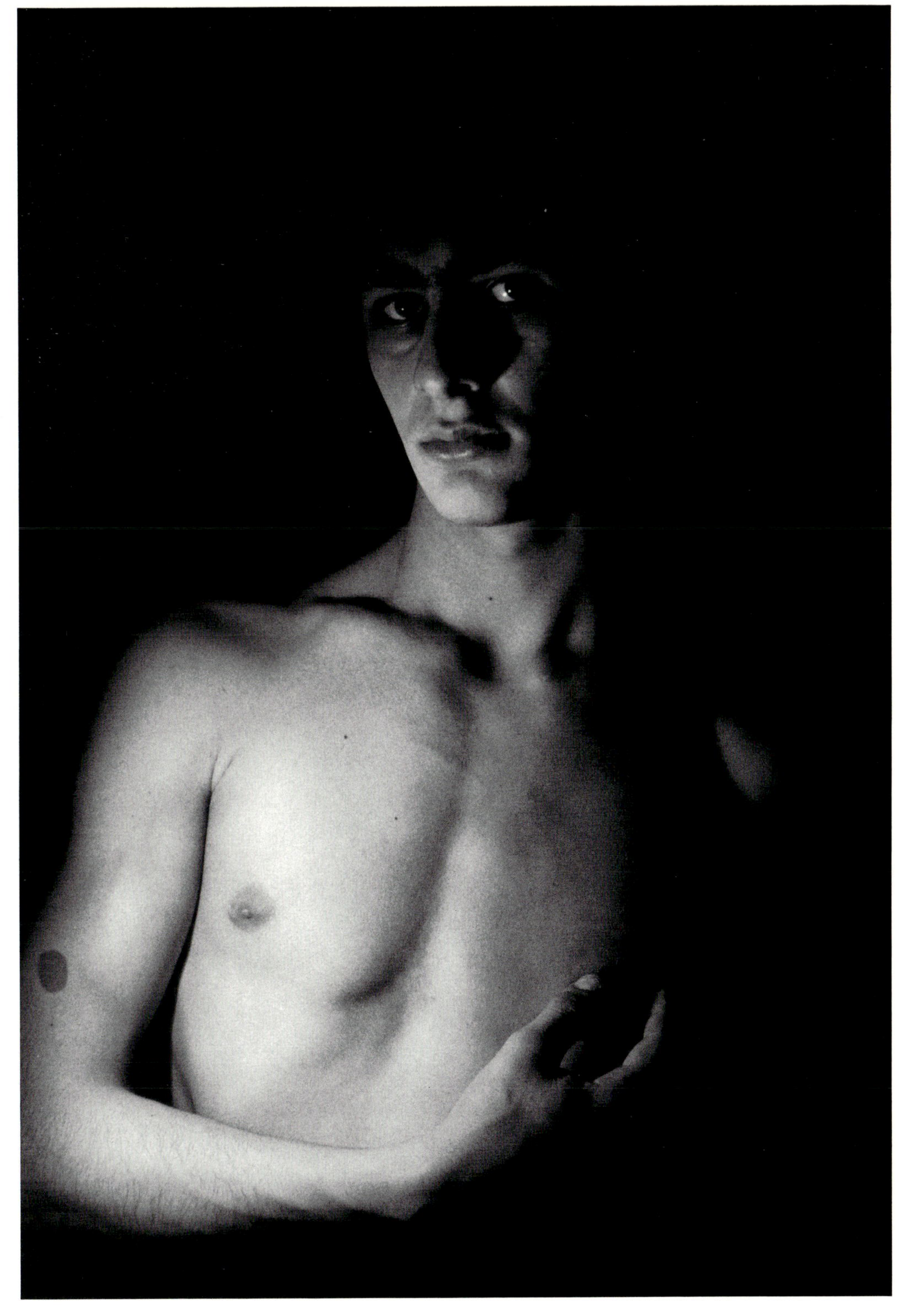

Roberto, 1985

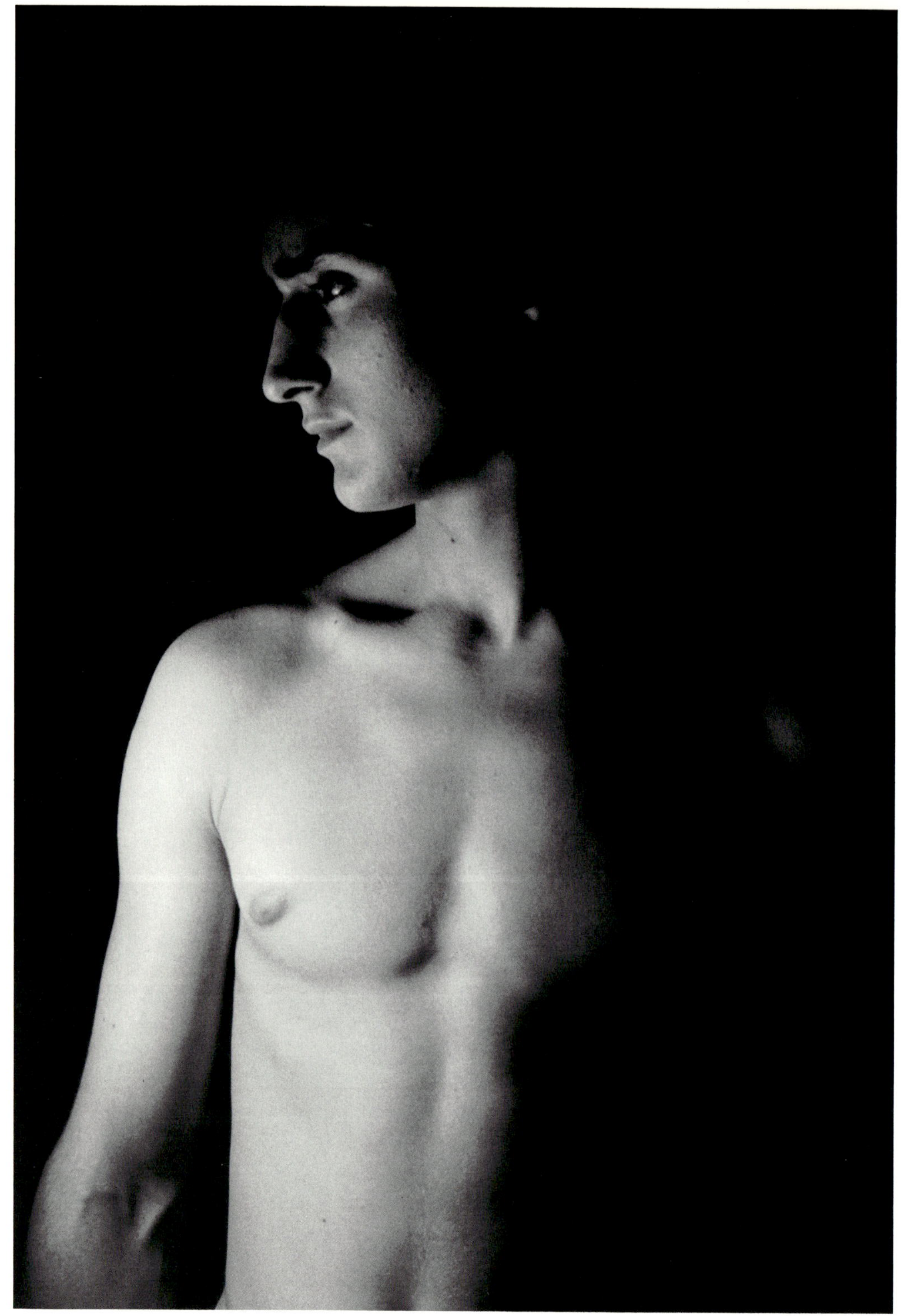

Davide, 1985

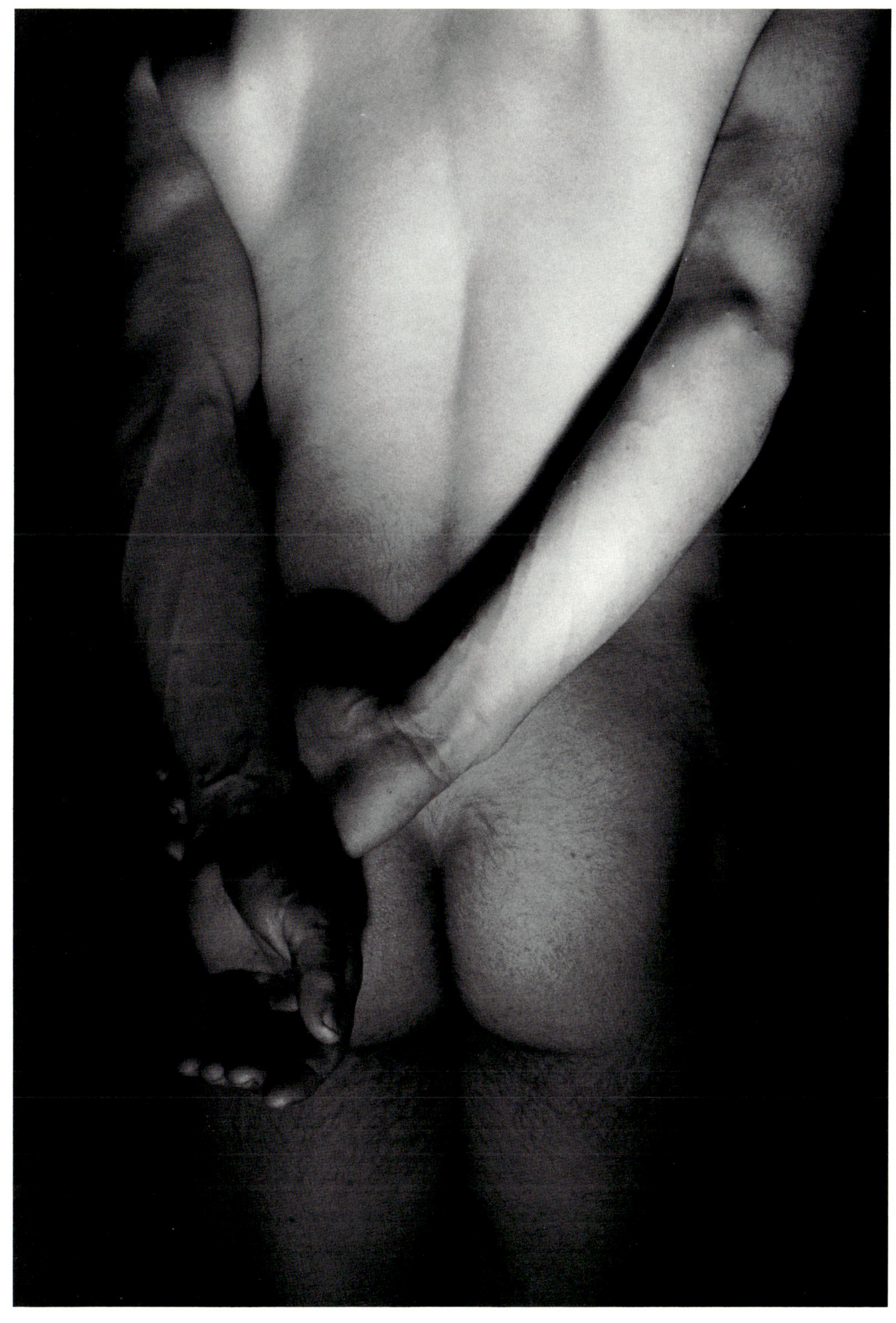

Gennaro, 1984

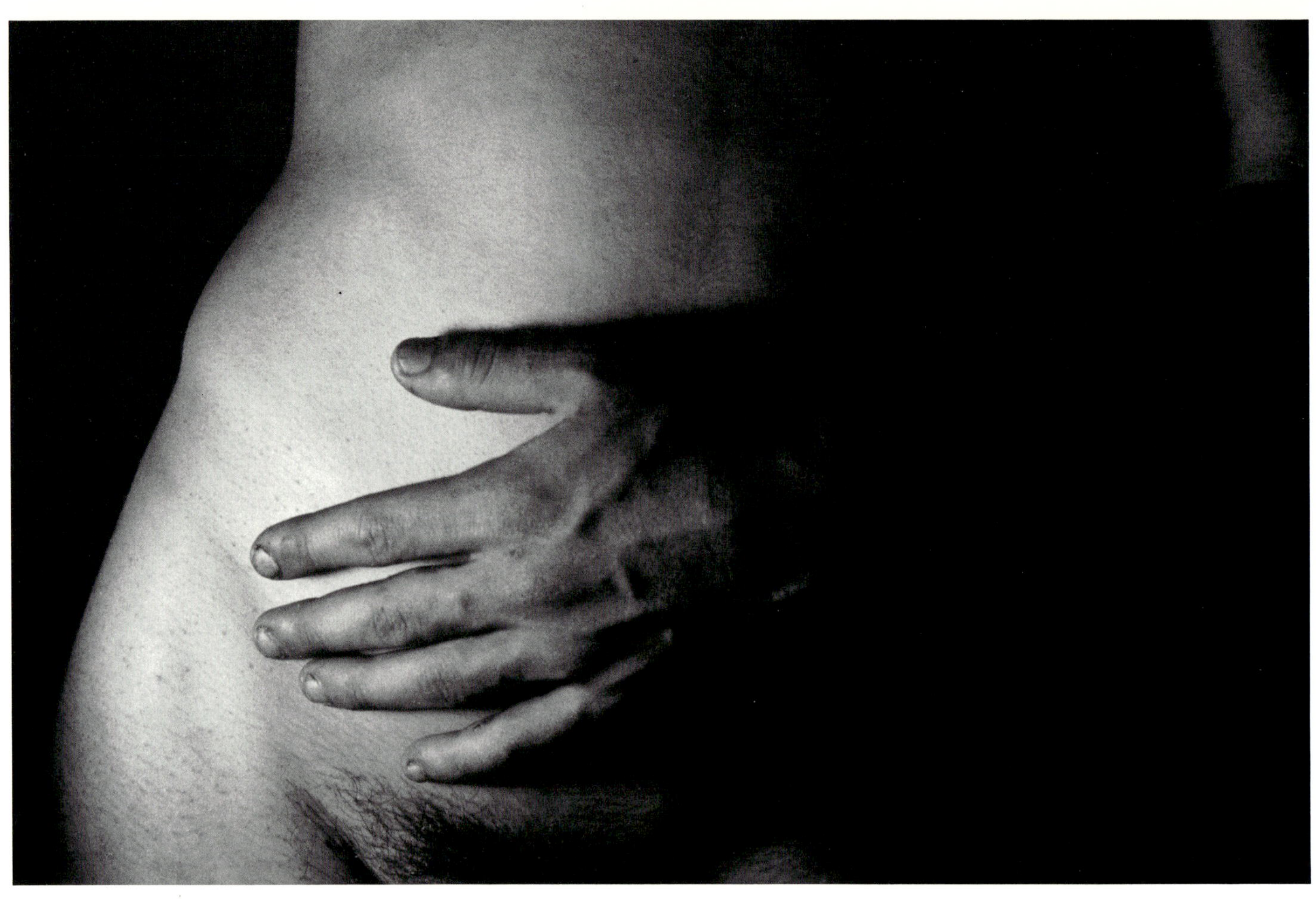

 Gennaro, 1984

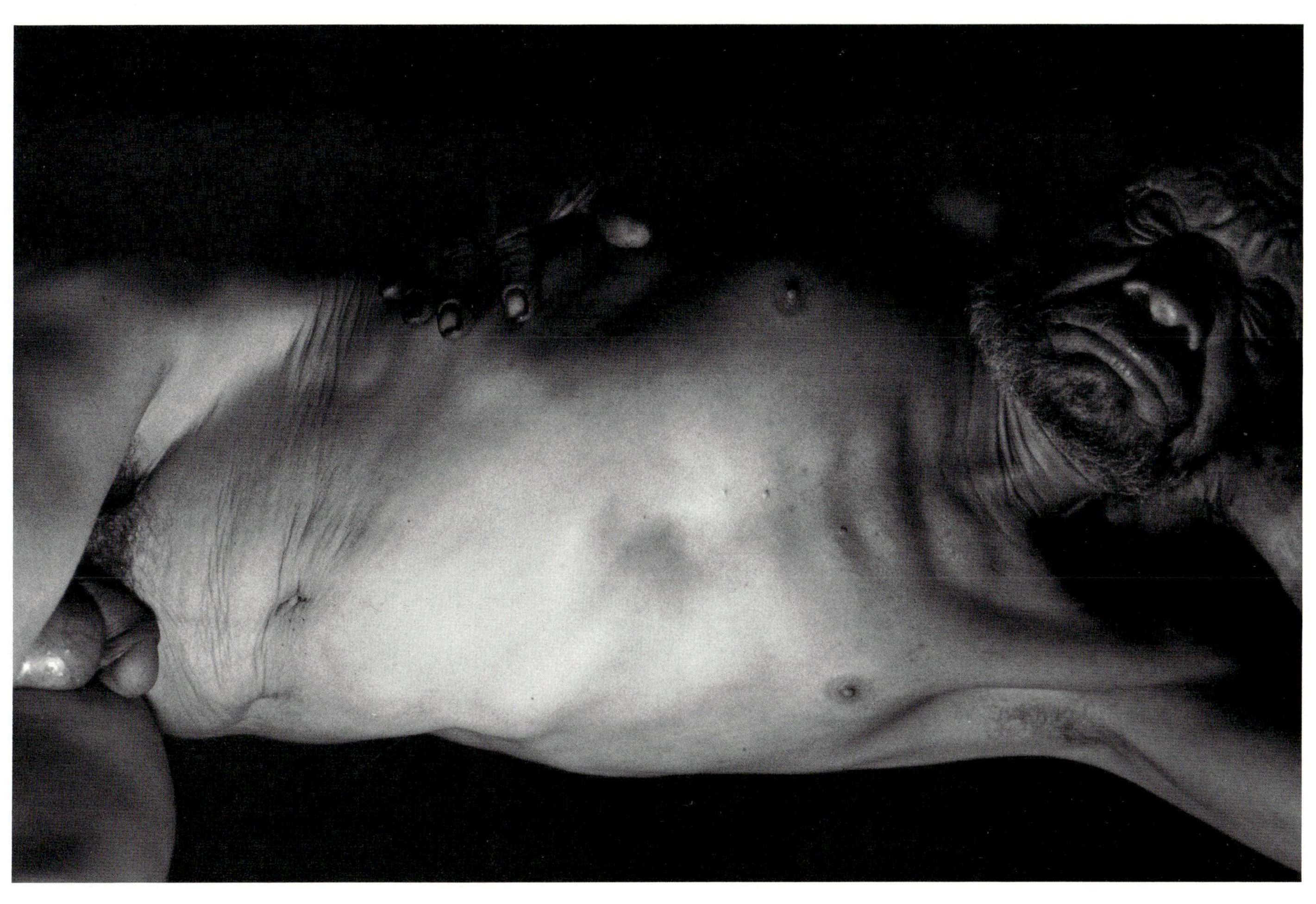

Umberto, 1983

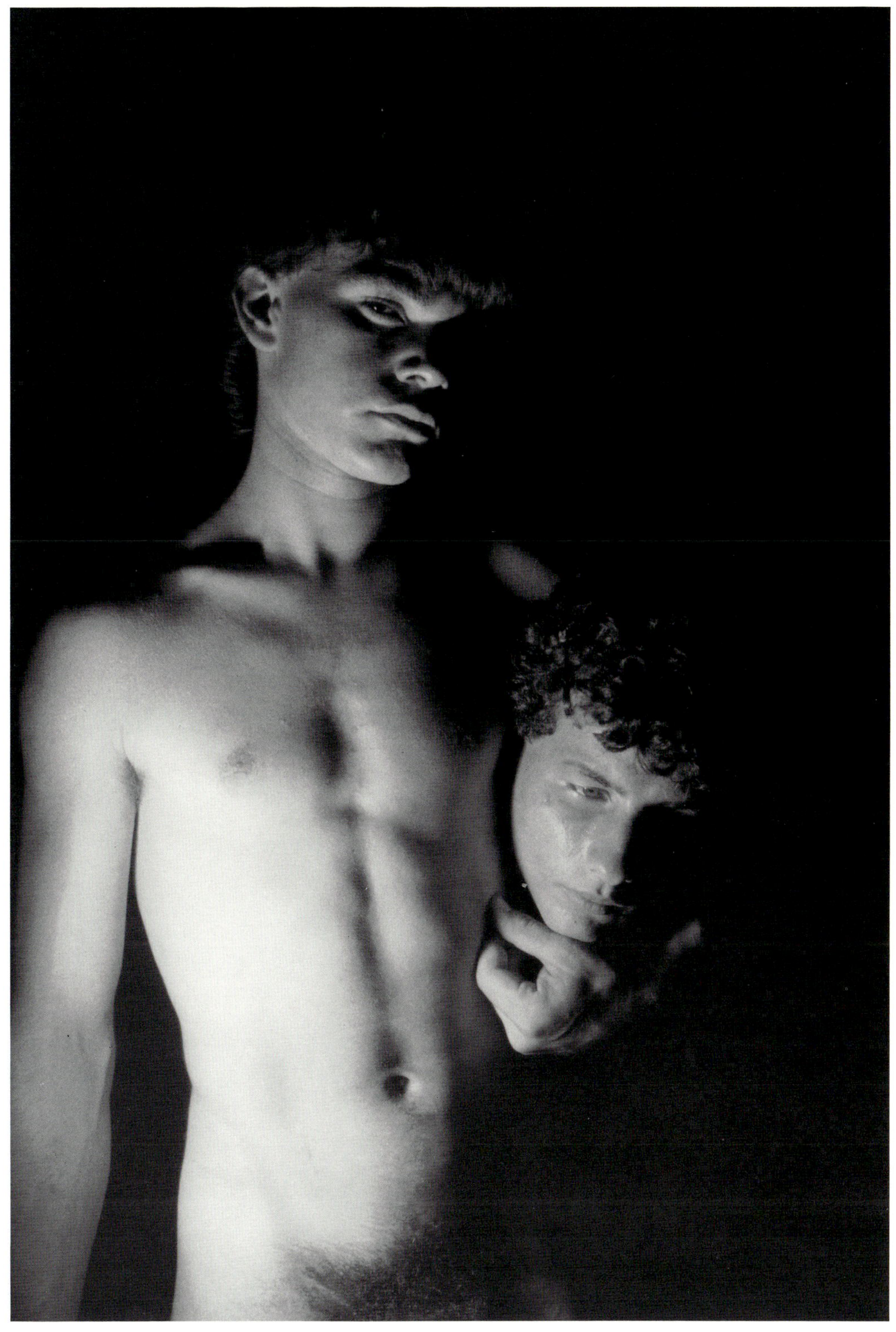

Davide e Goliath, 1985

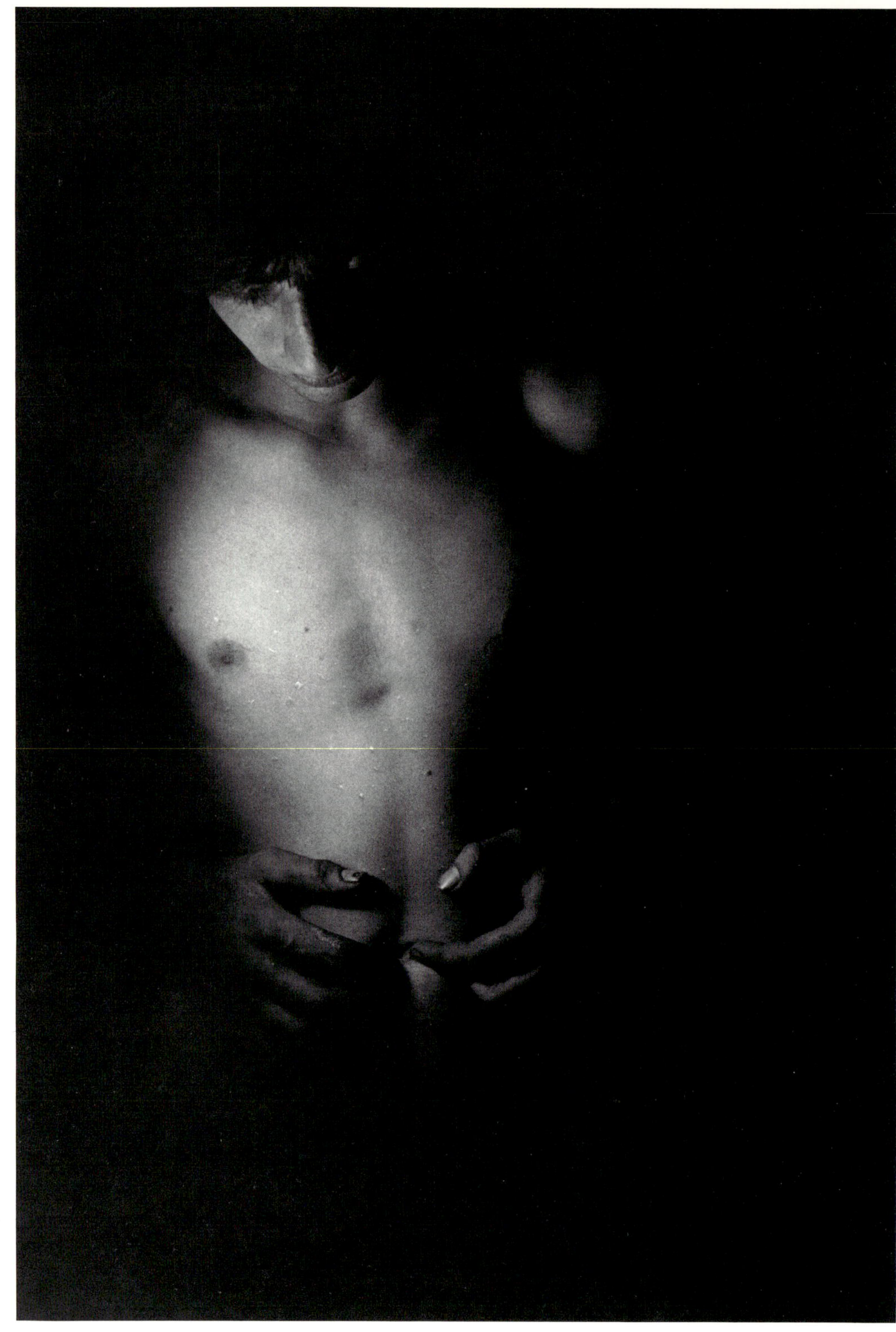

Gianni, 1985

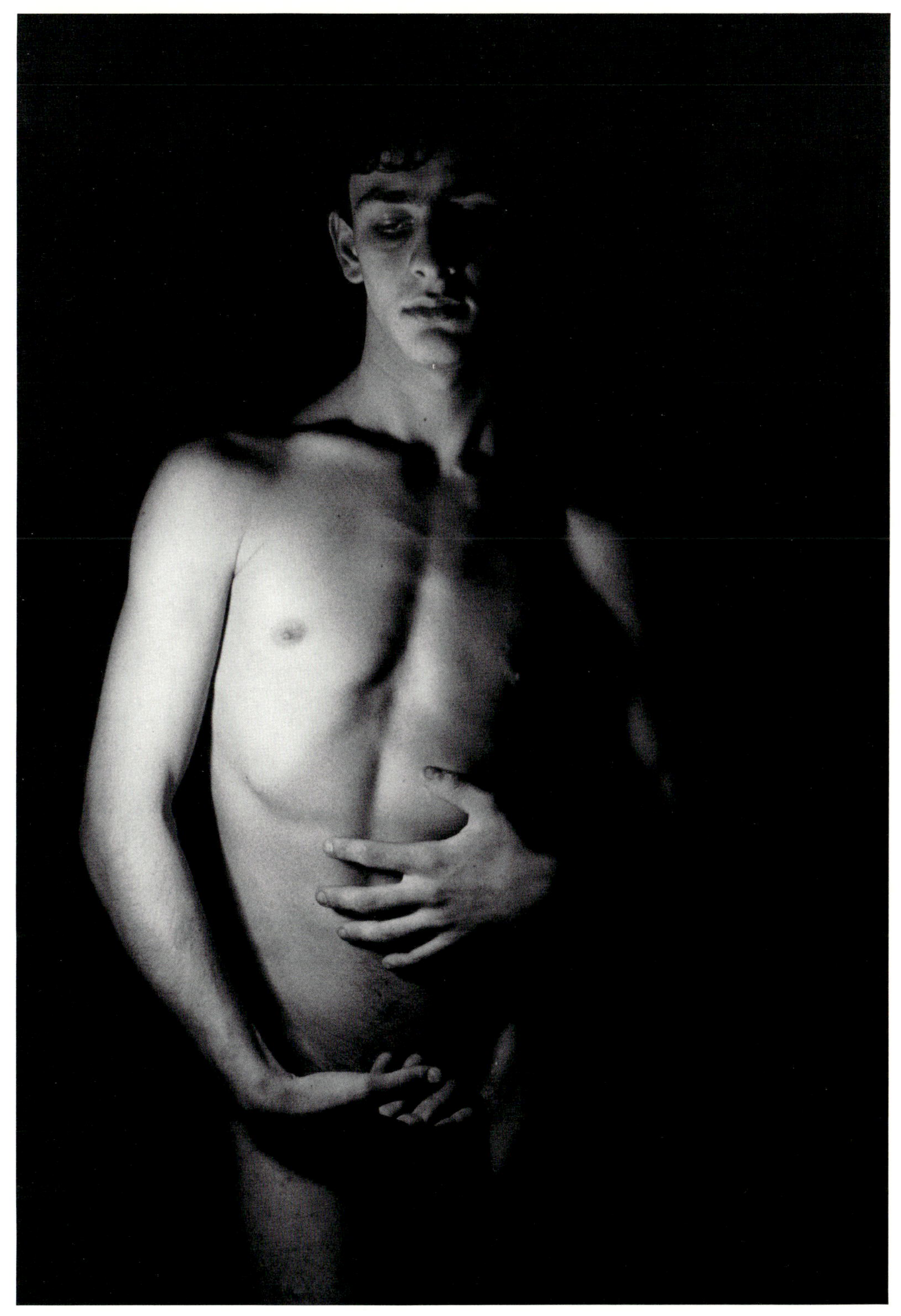

Roberto, 1985

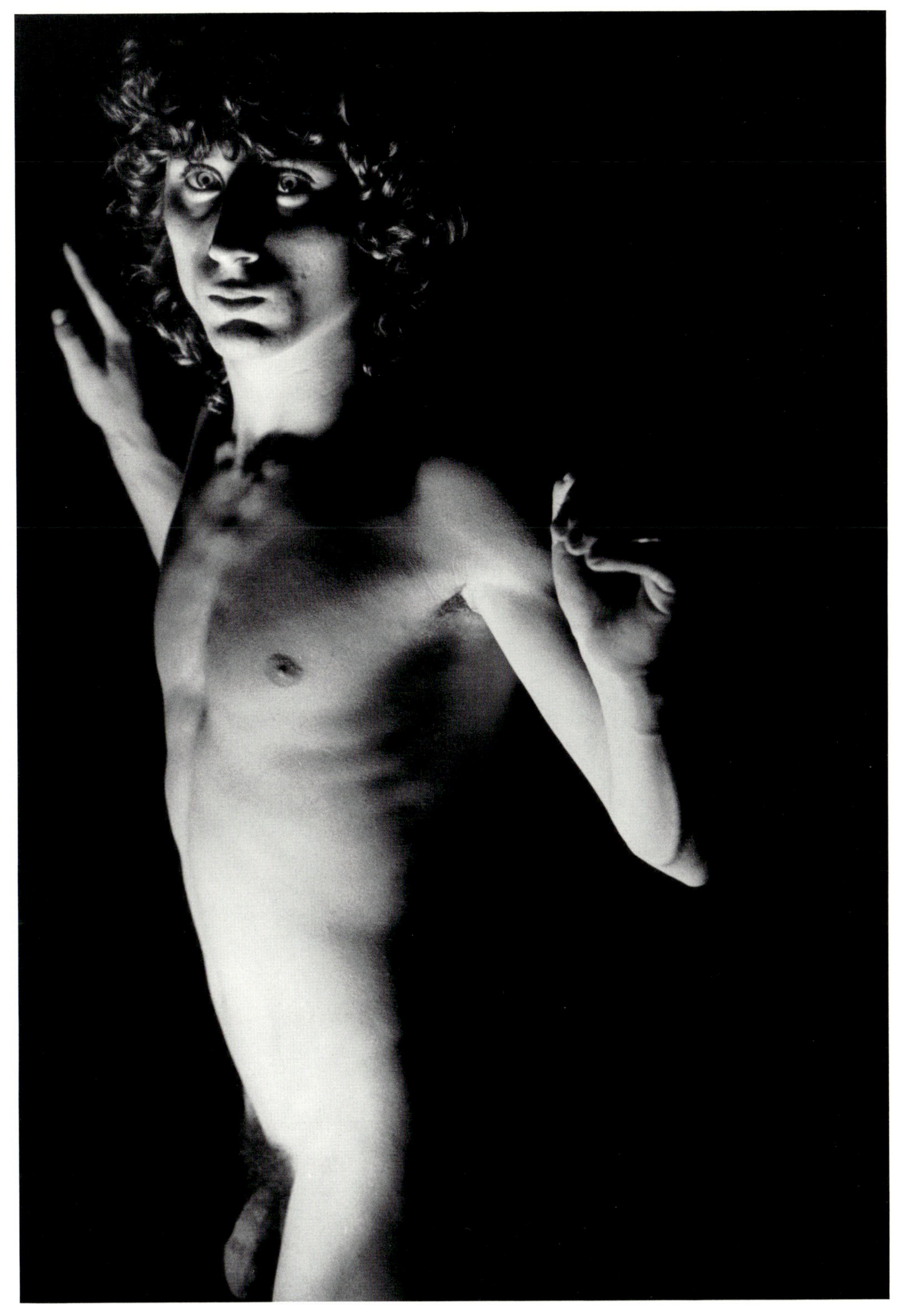

Edoardo, 1984

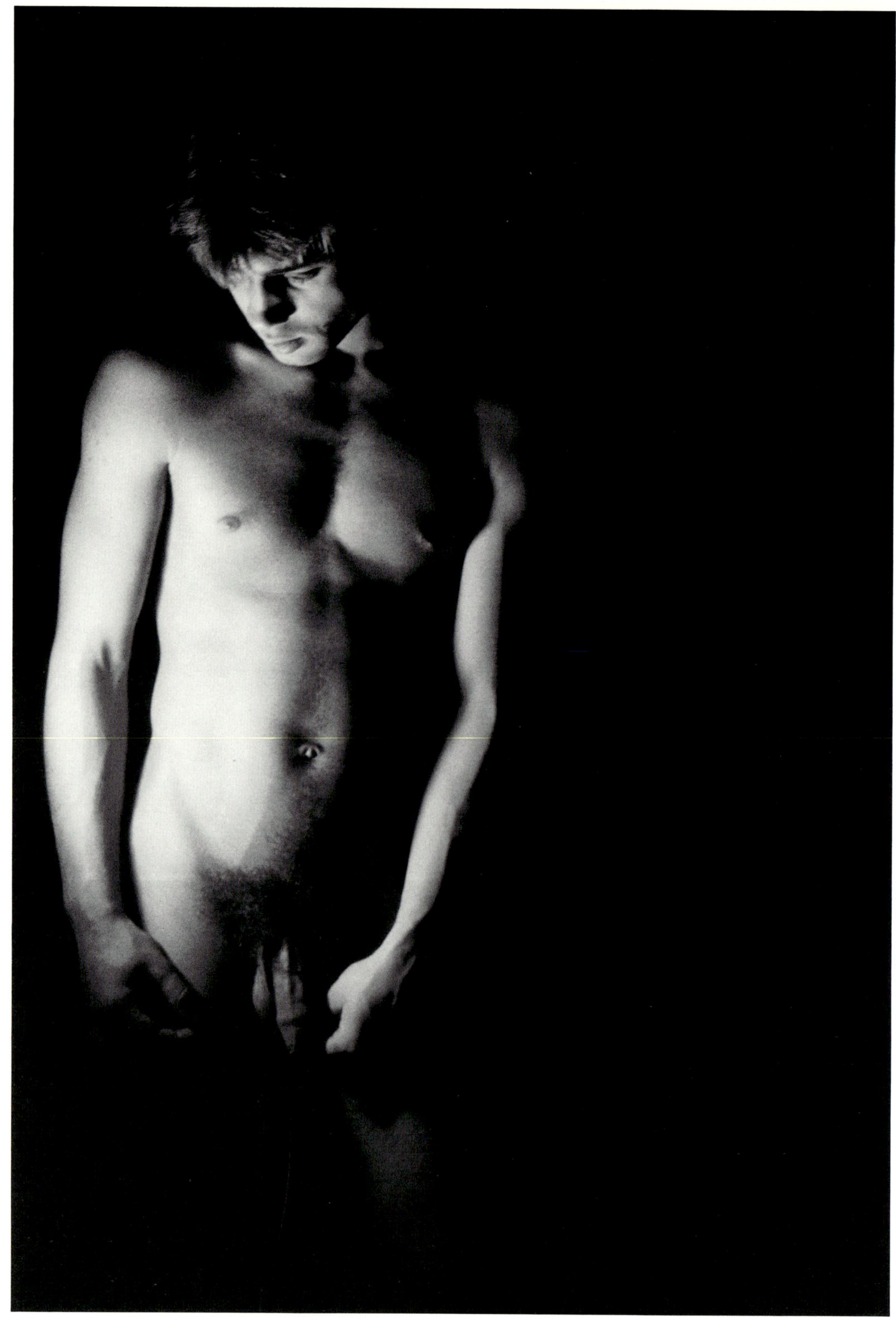

Arturo, 1985

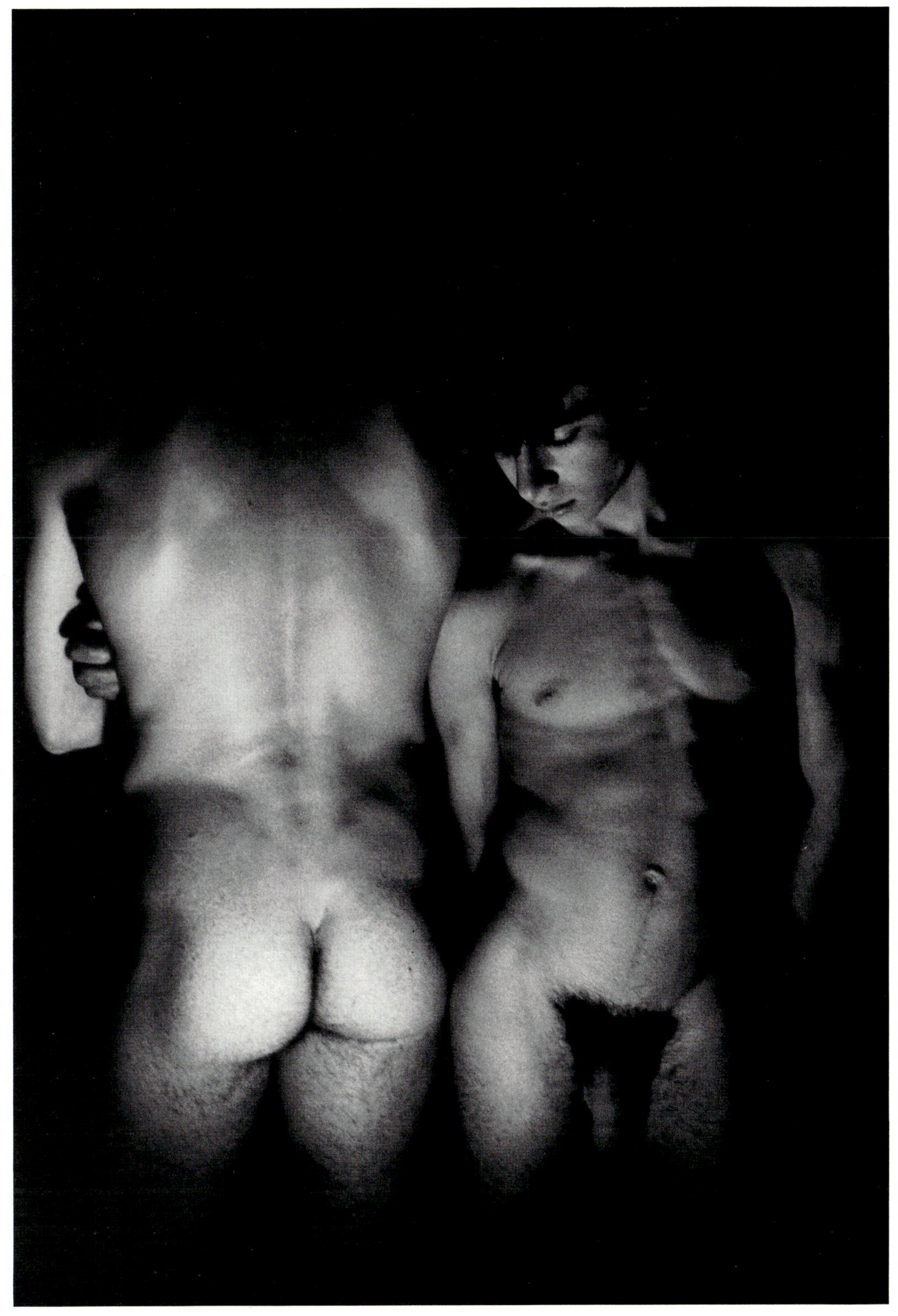

Gli Fratelli Romolo e Claudio, 1984

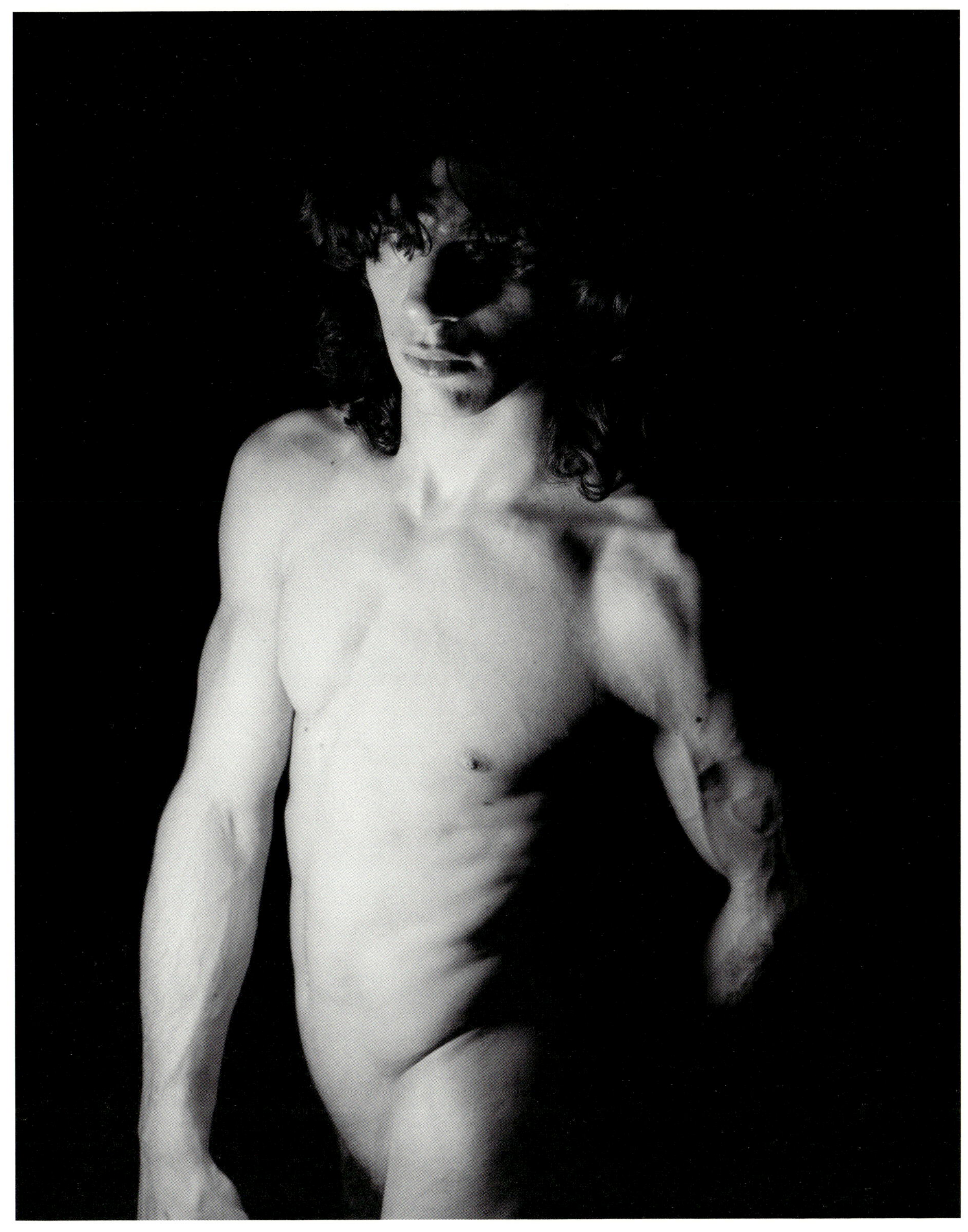

Pino, 1987

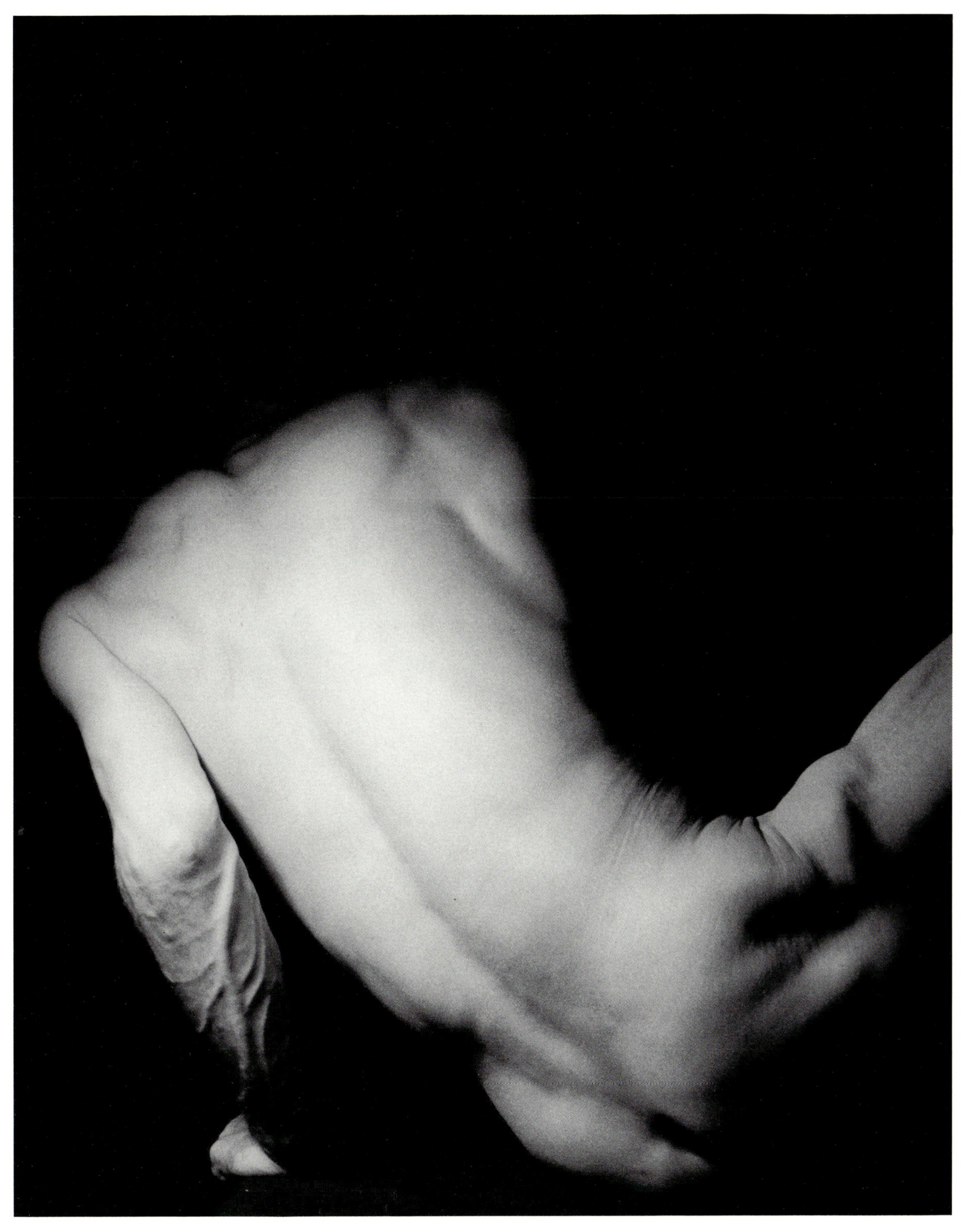

Rudolf Nureyev, 1984

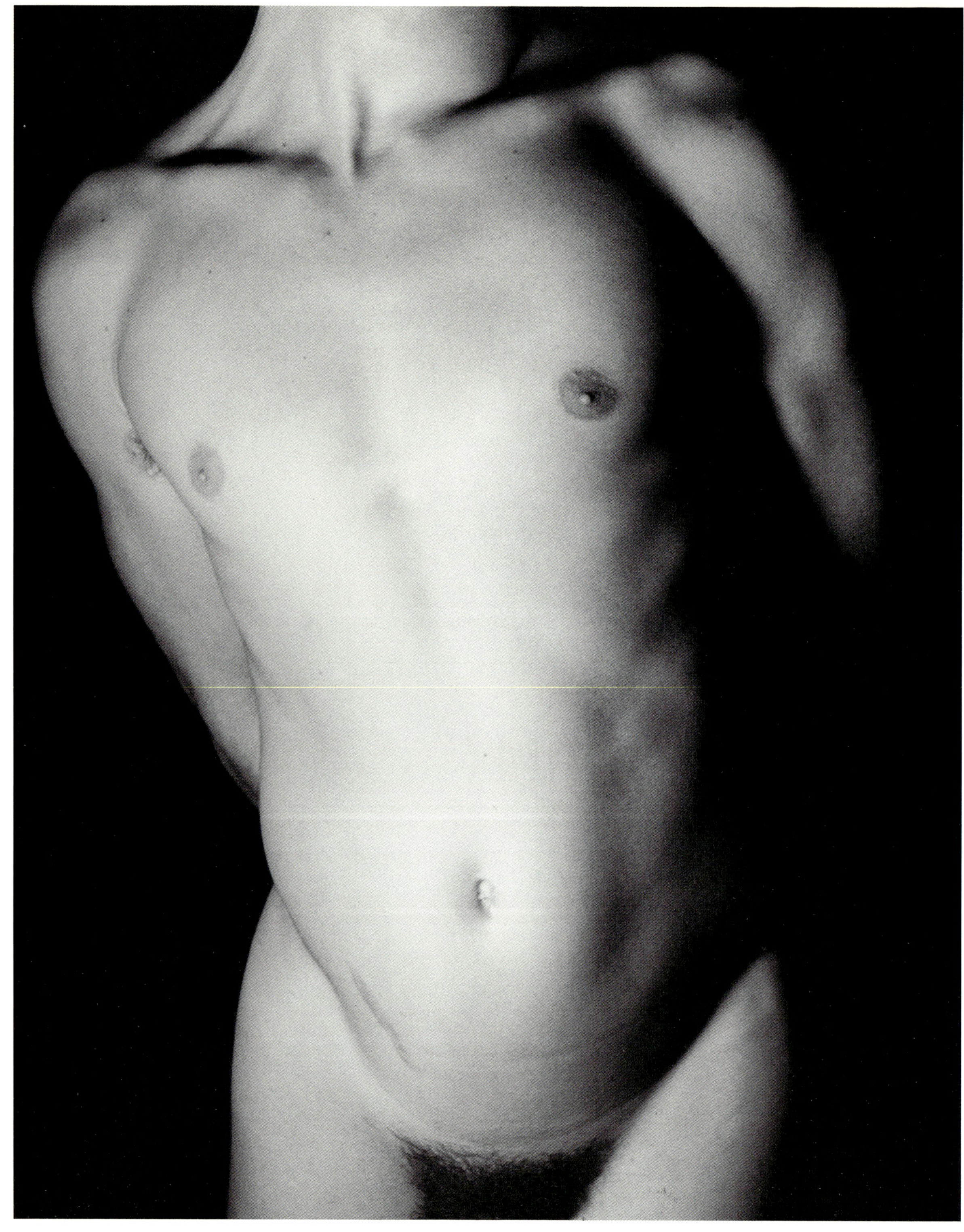

Ivo, 1987

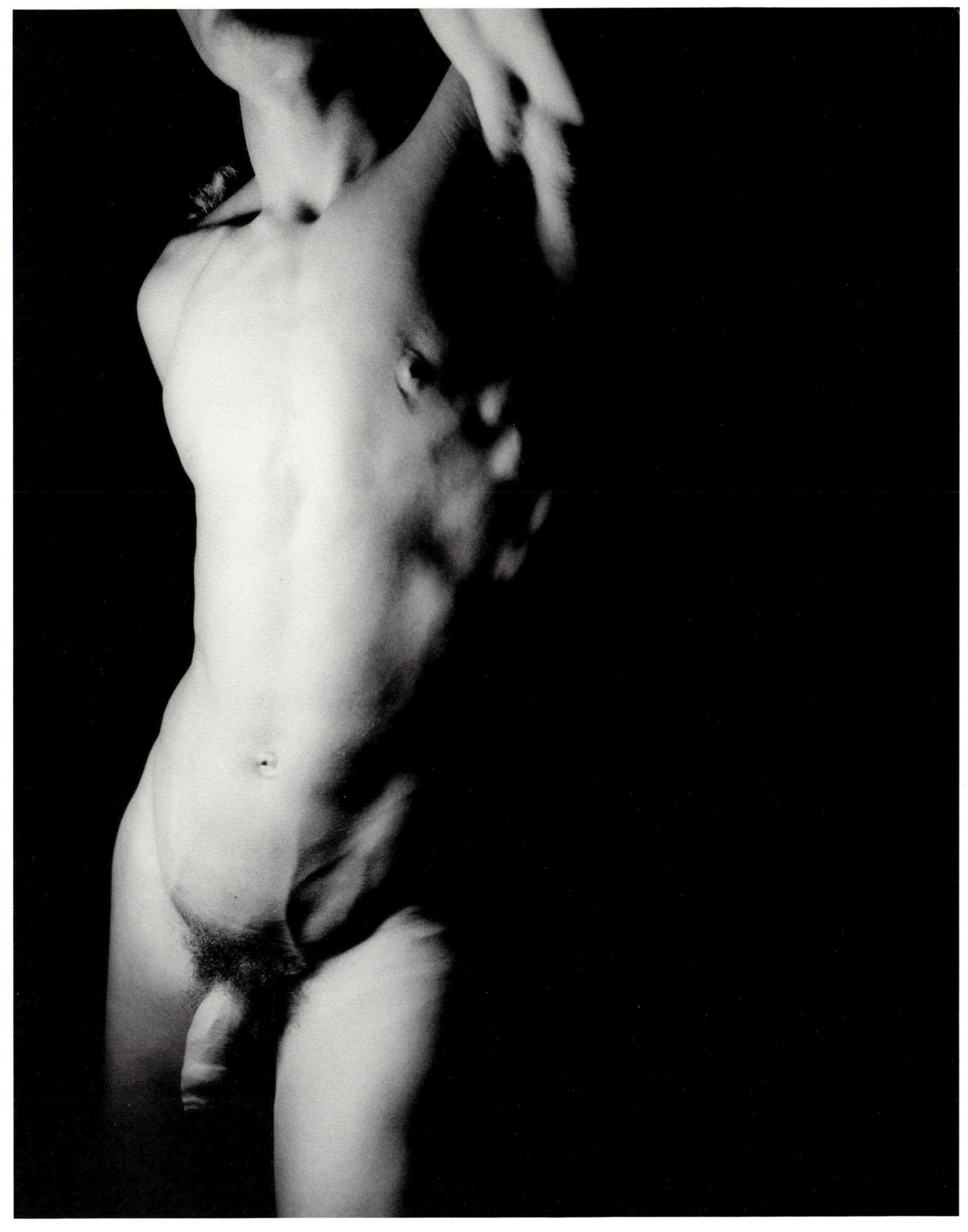

Torsione, 1989

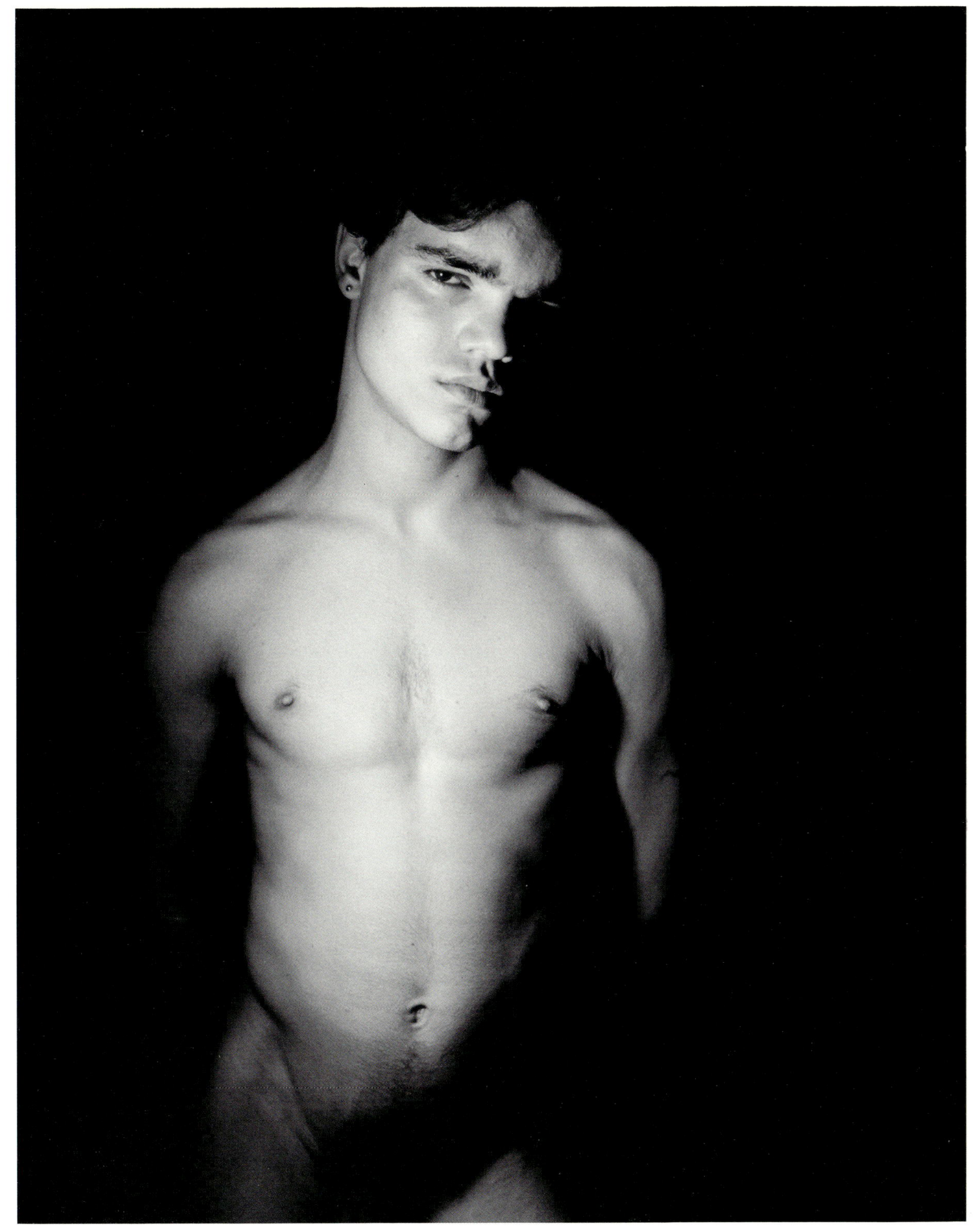

Augusto, 1989

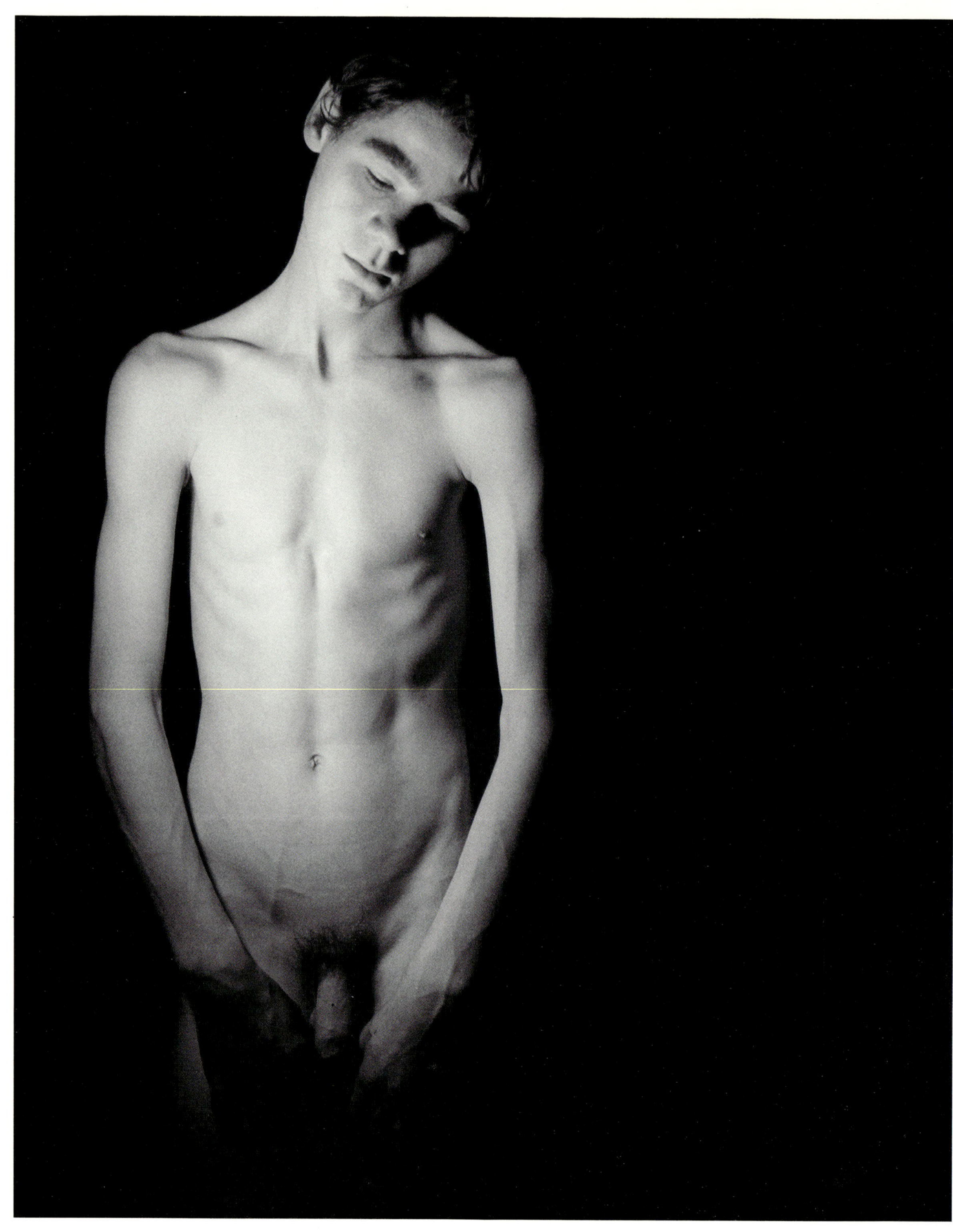

 Omaggio al Giovane Werther 2, 1989

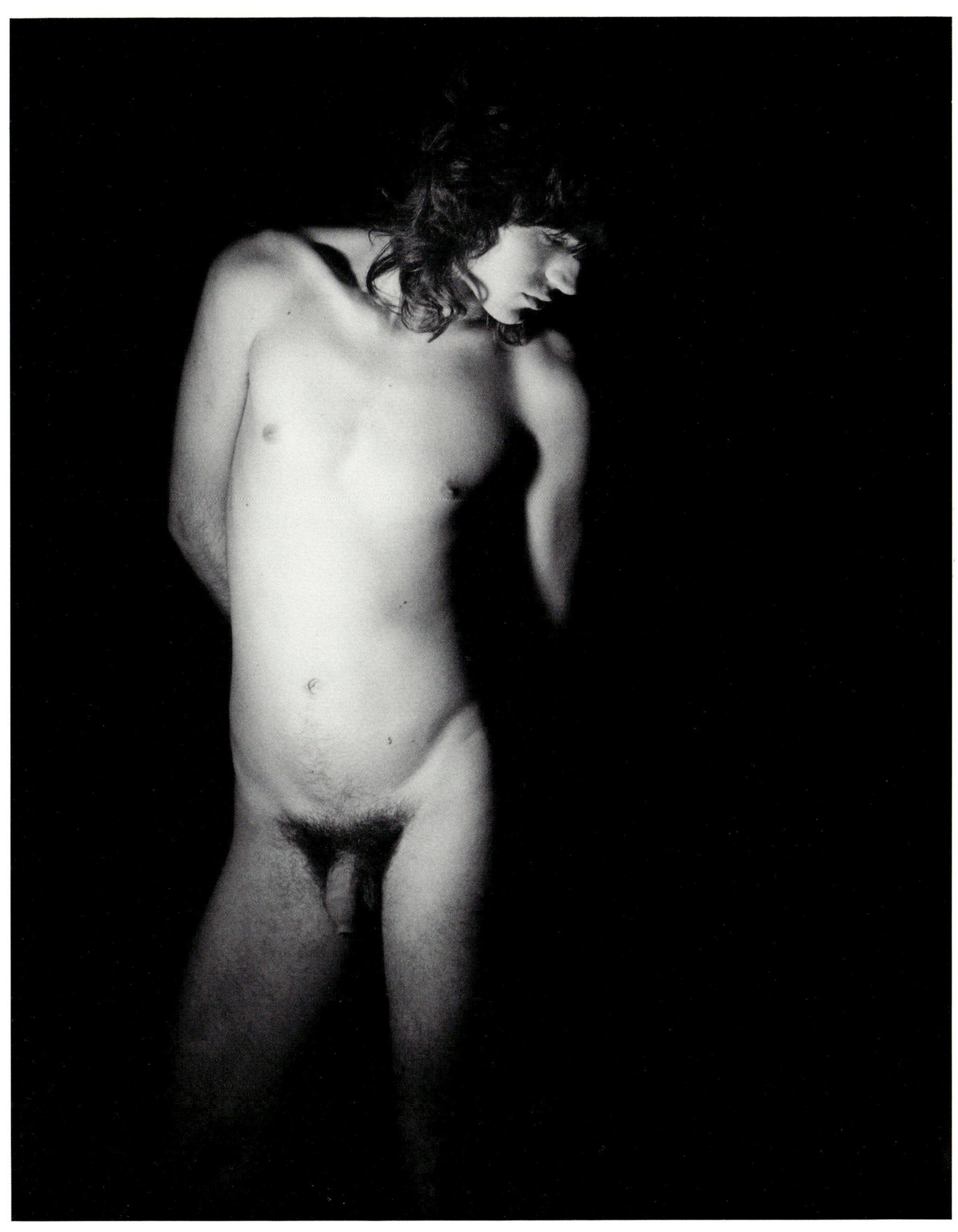

Omaggio al Giovane Werther 1, 1987

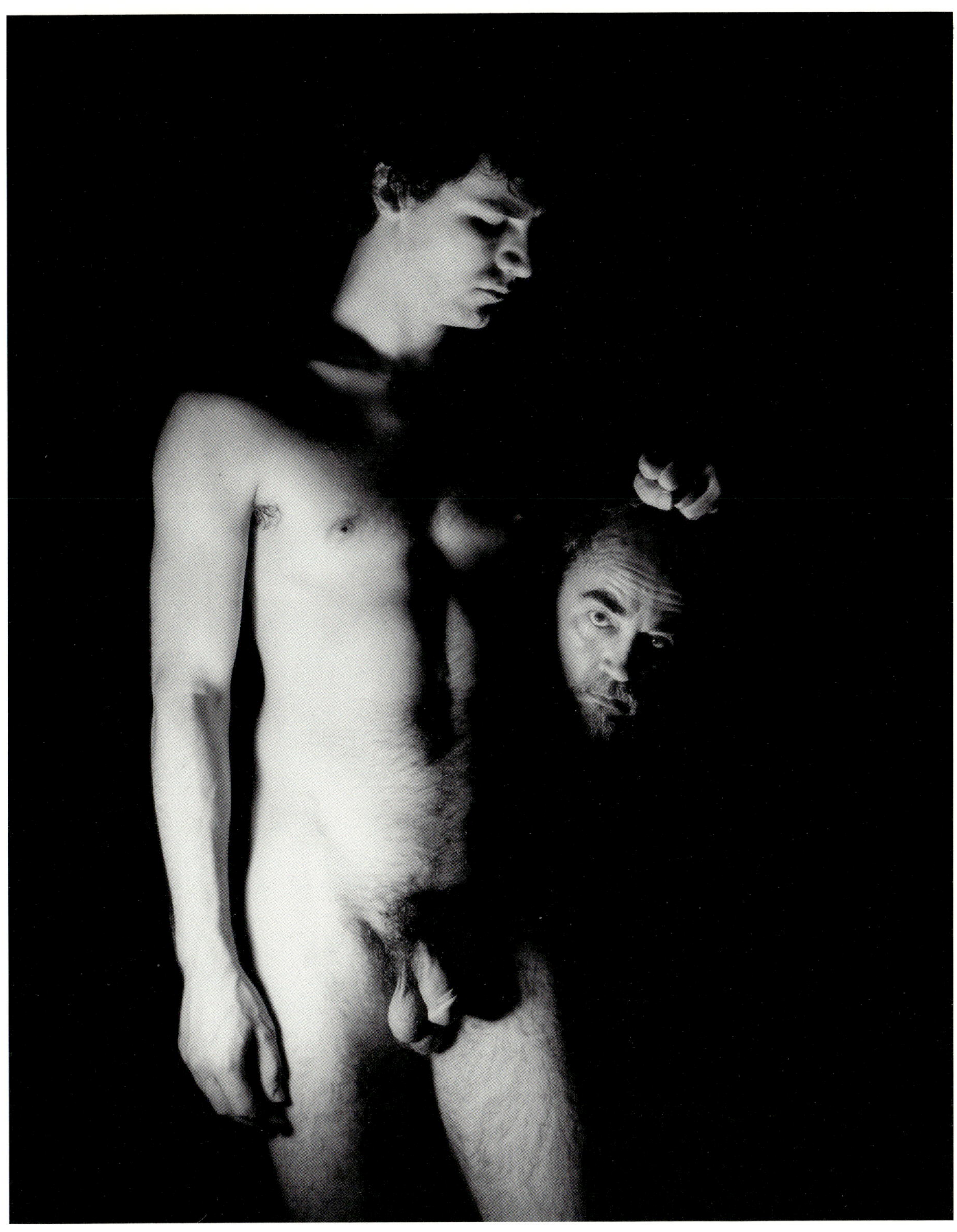

Autoritratto Immaginario, 1989

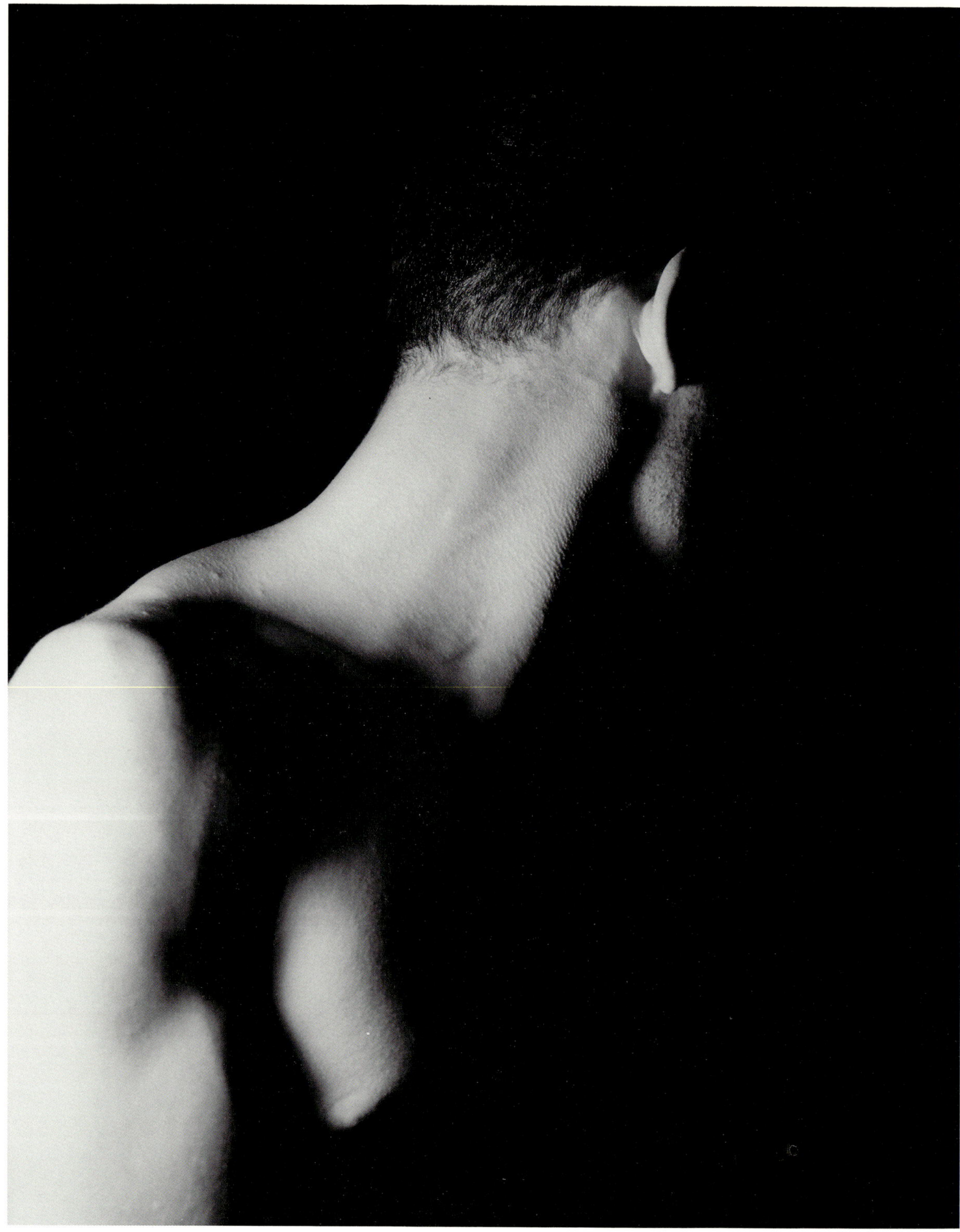

Ettore, 1989

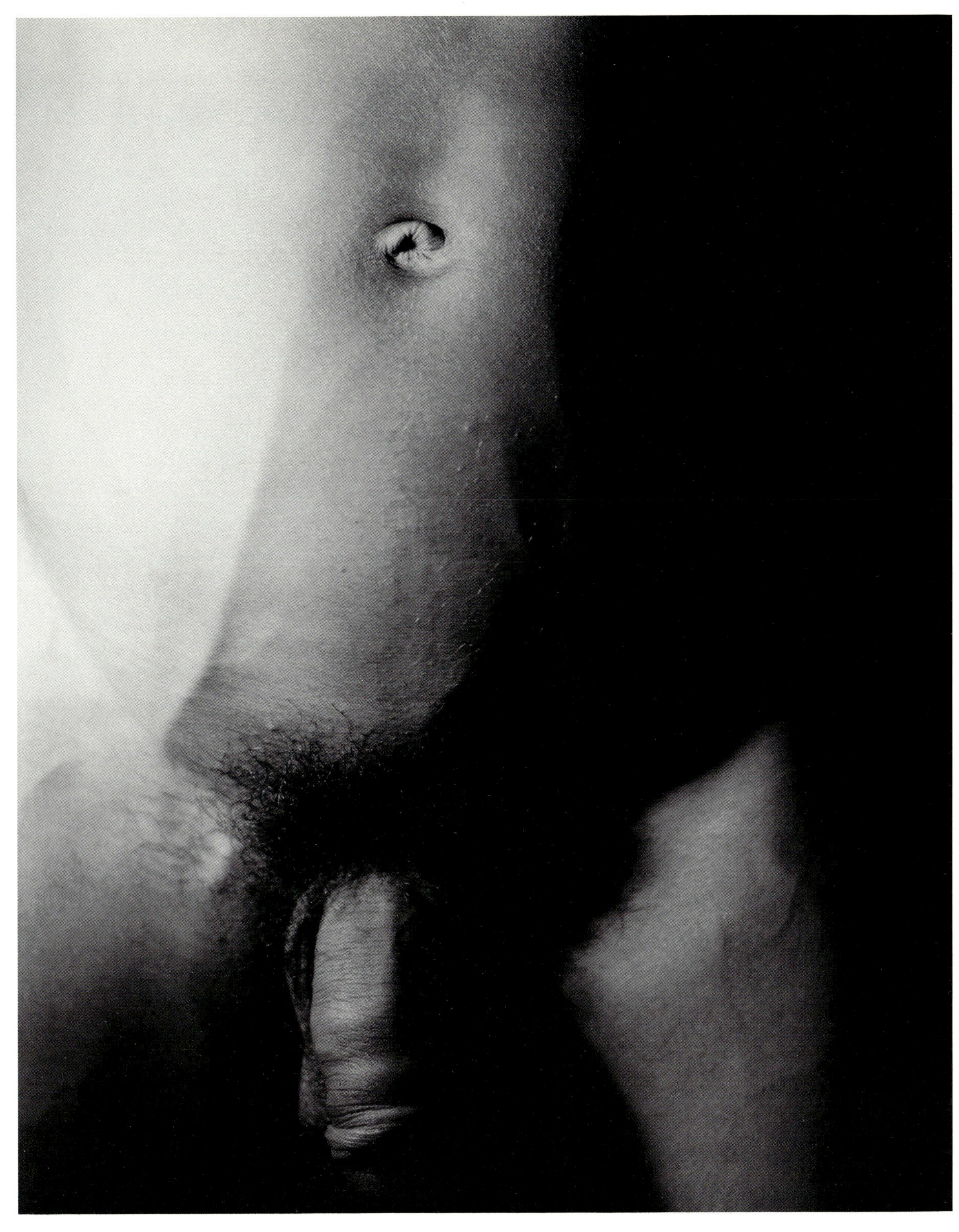

Fertilità, 1989

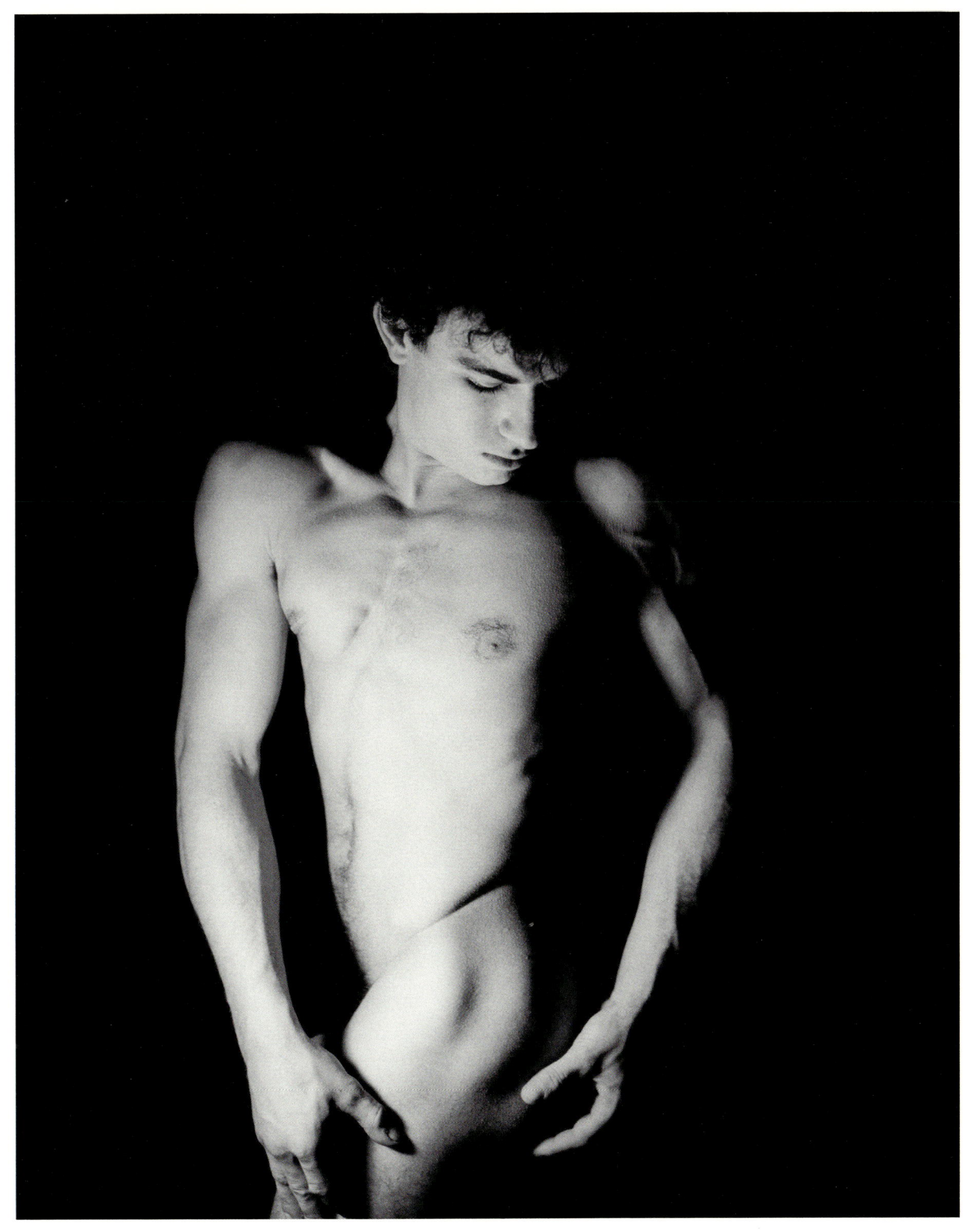

Claudio, 1987

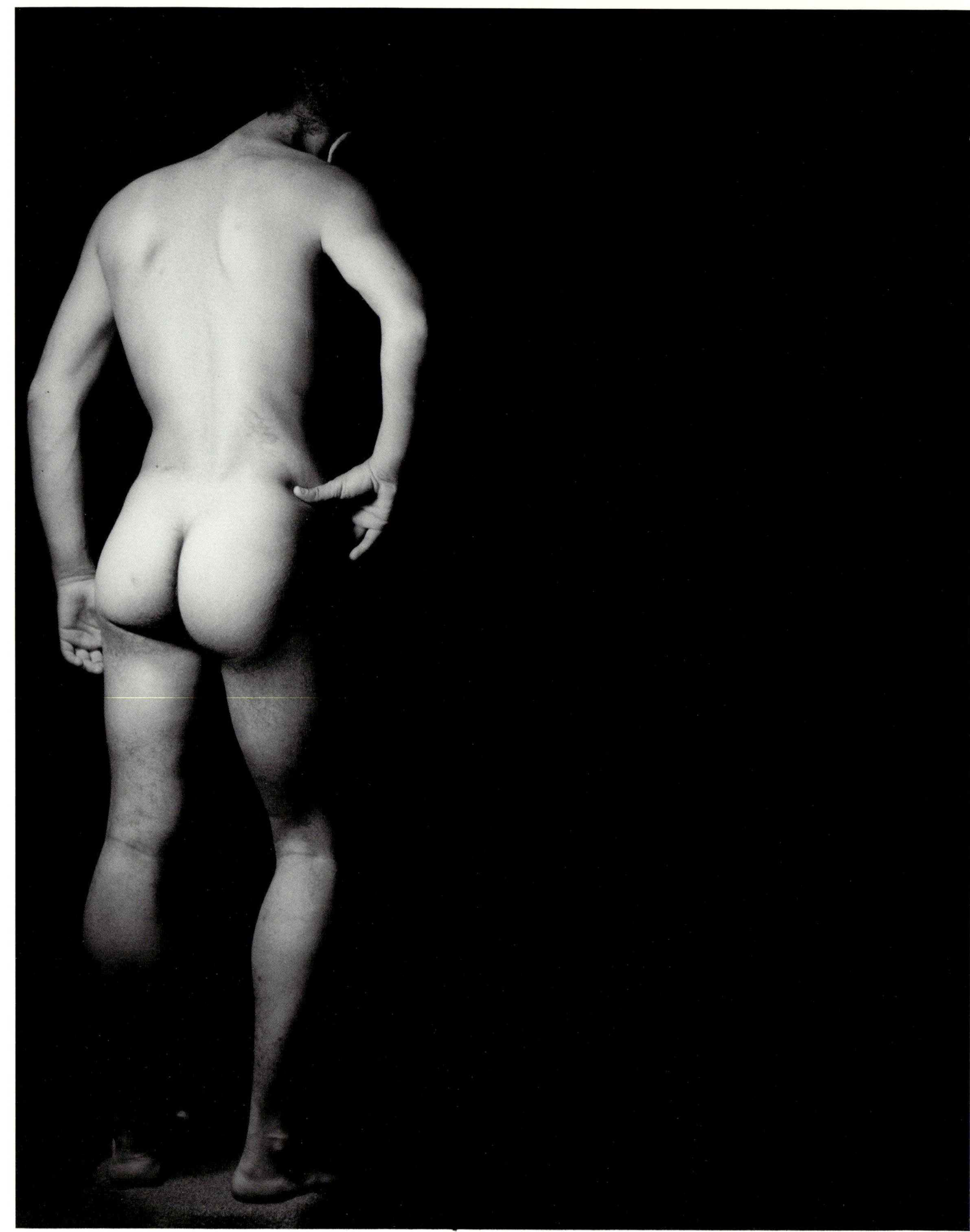

Mercurio, 1993

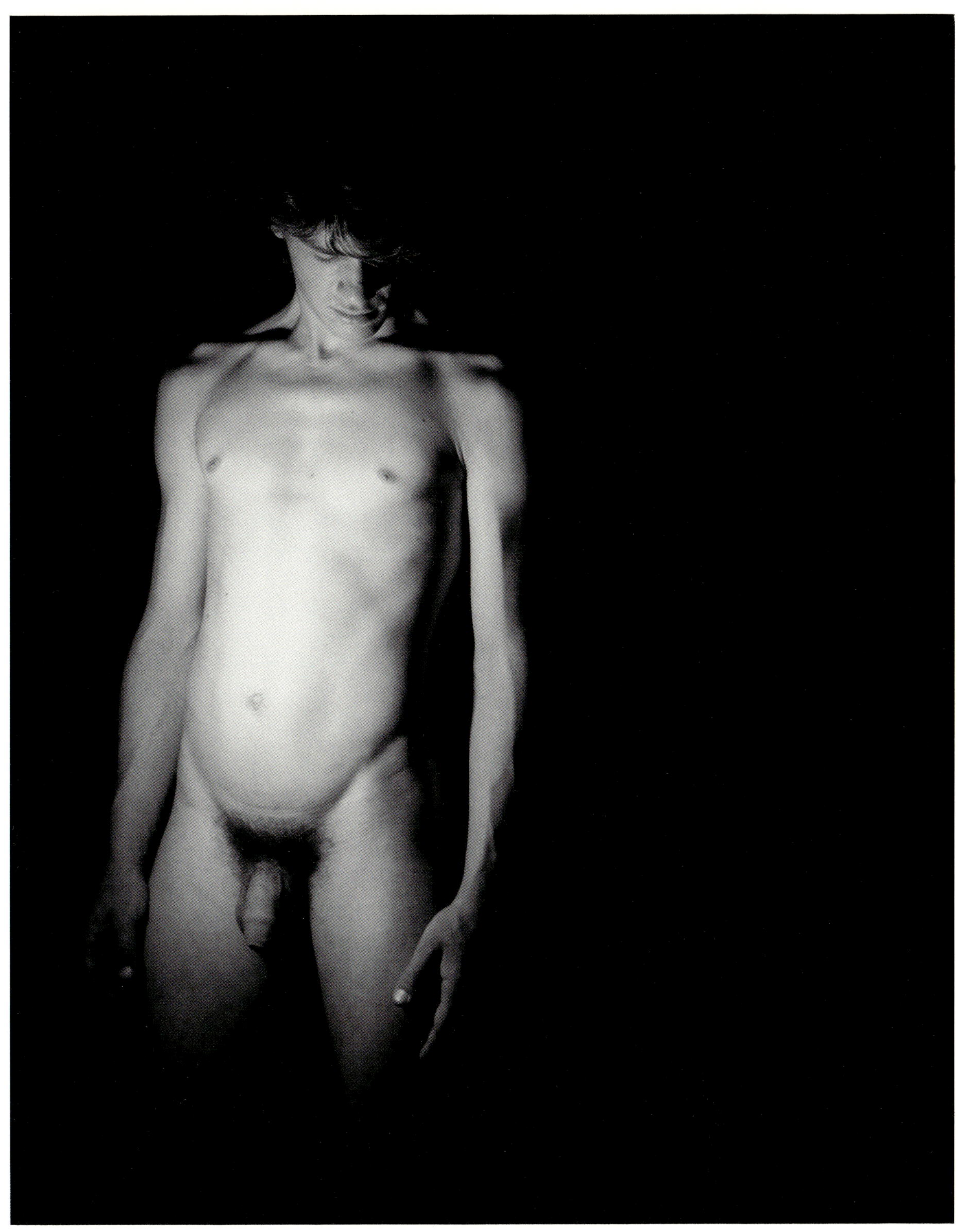

Ragazzo di Trani, 1989

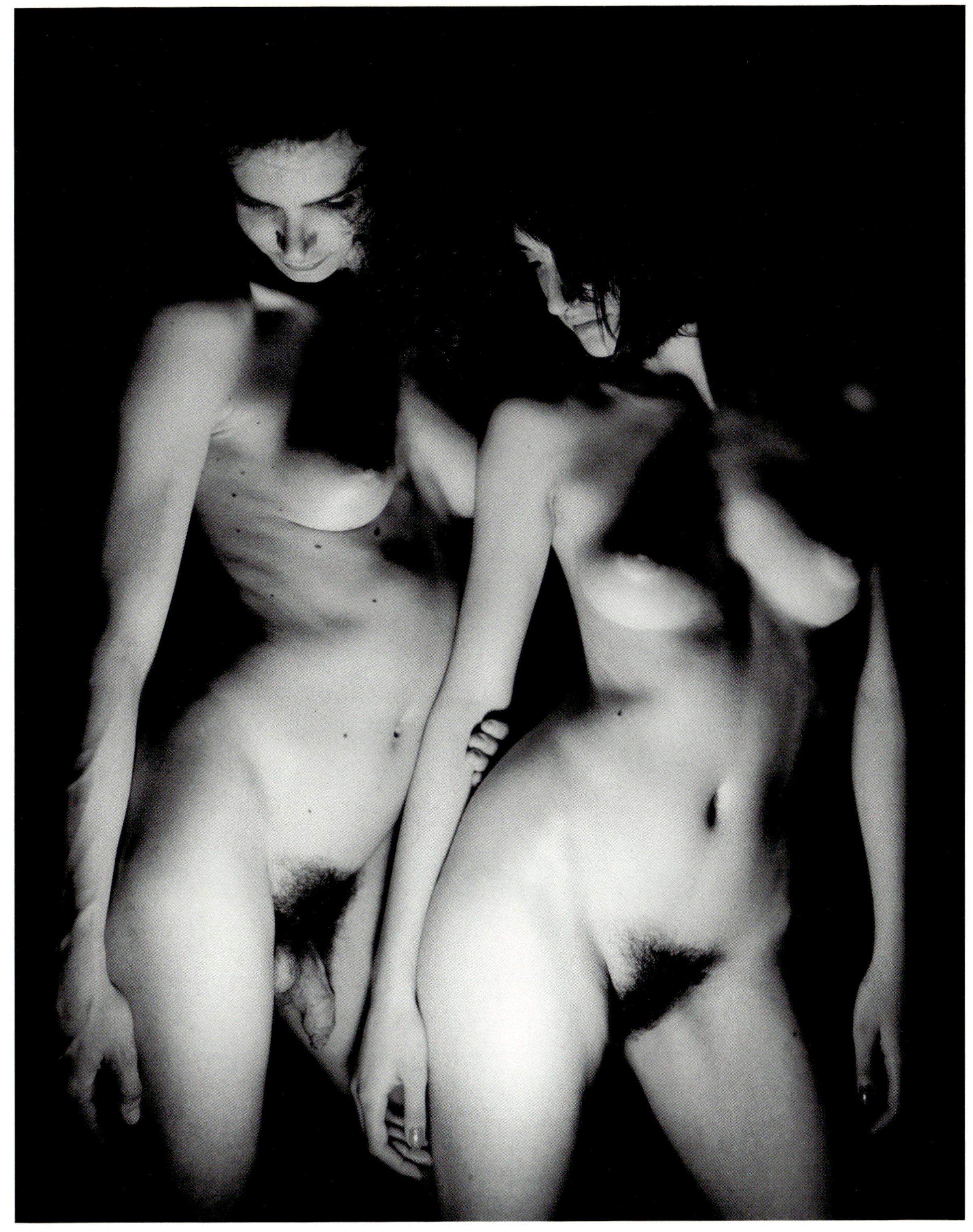

Metamorfosi, 1990

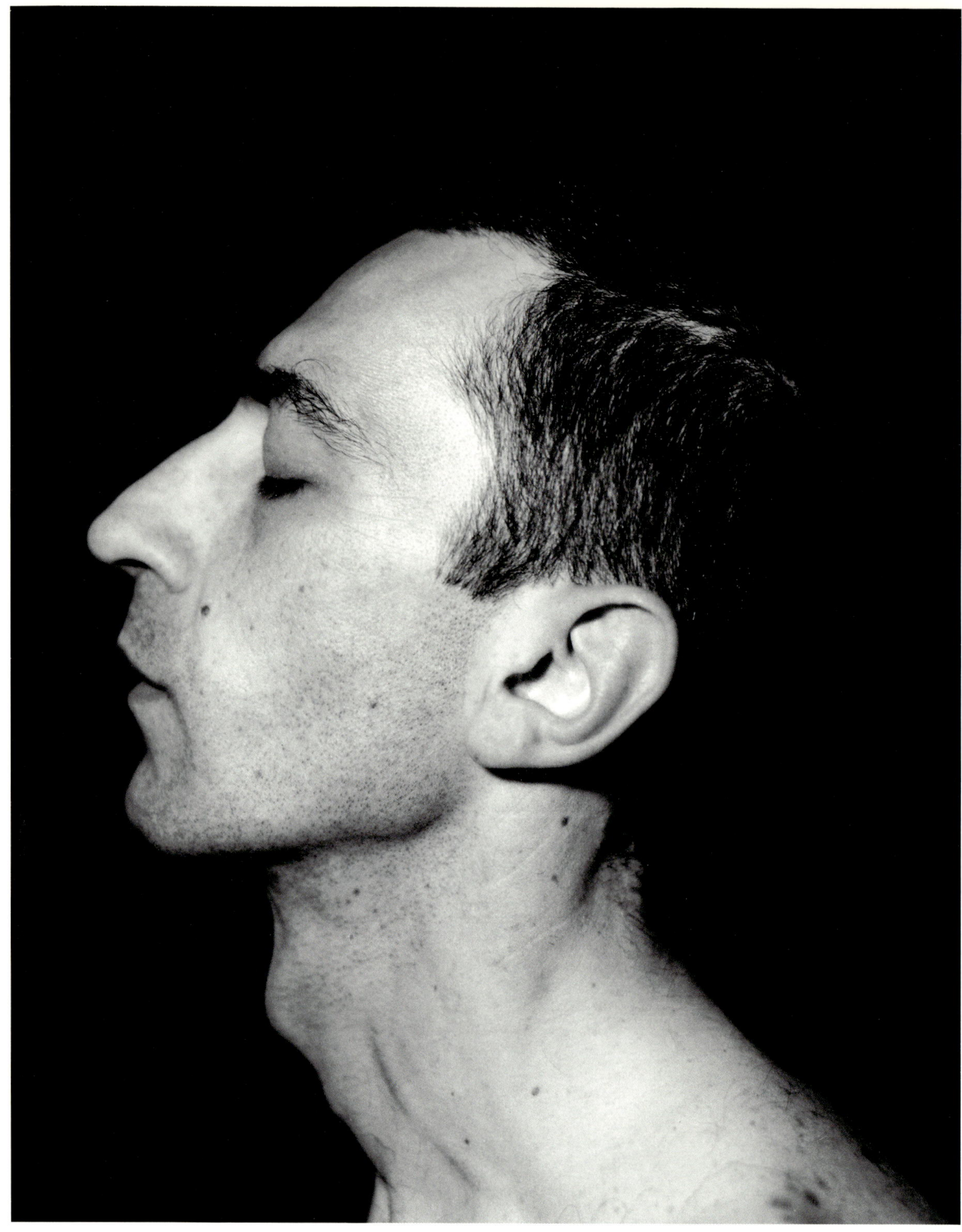

Oliviero, 1992

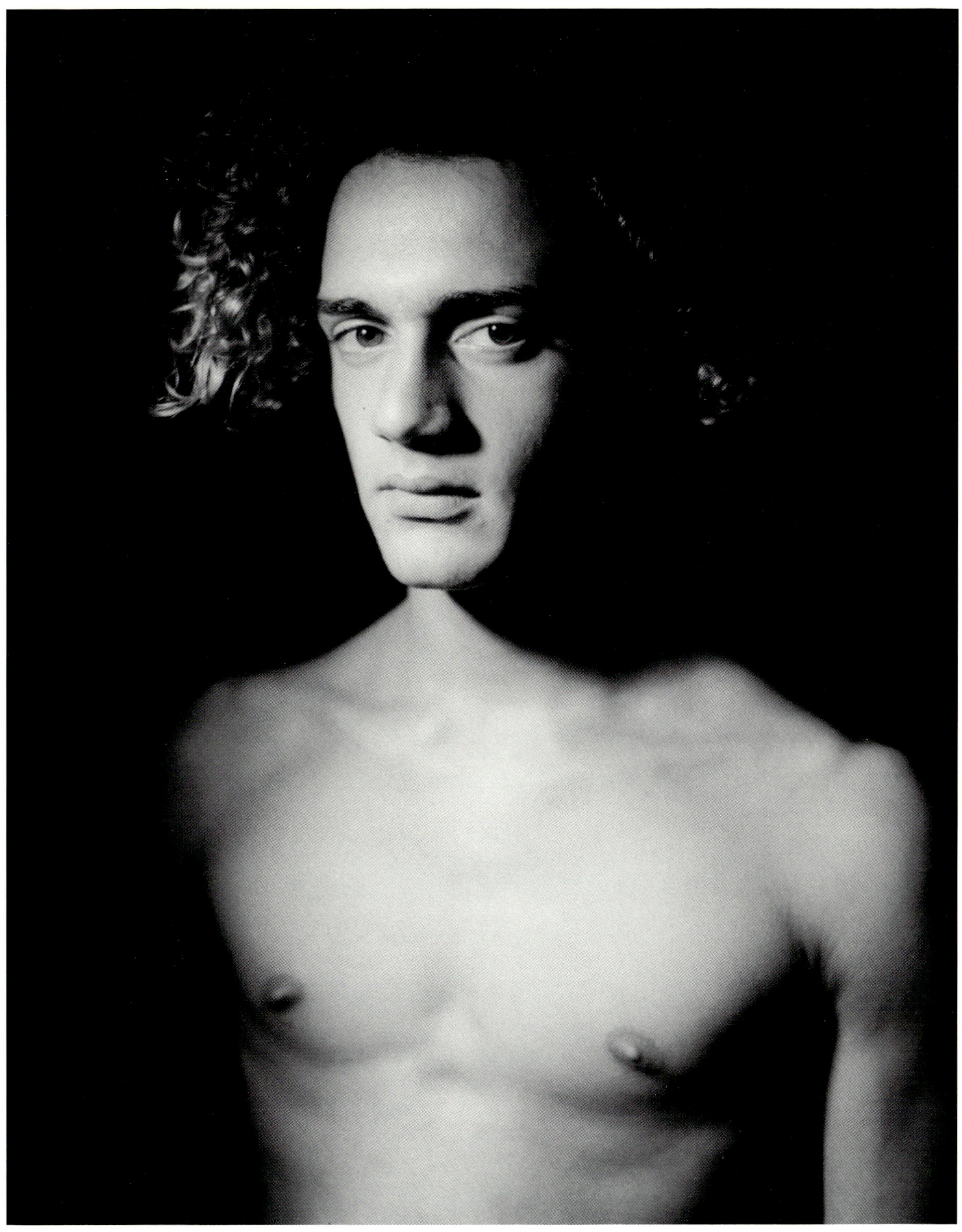

Giovane di S. Paolo di Civitate, 1991

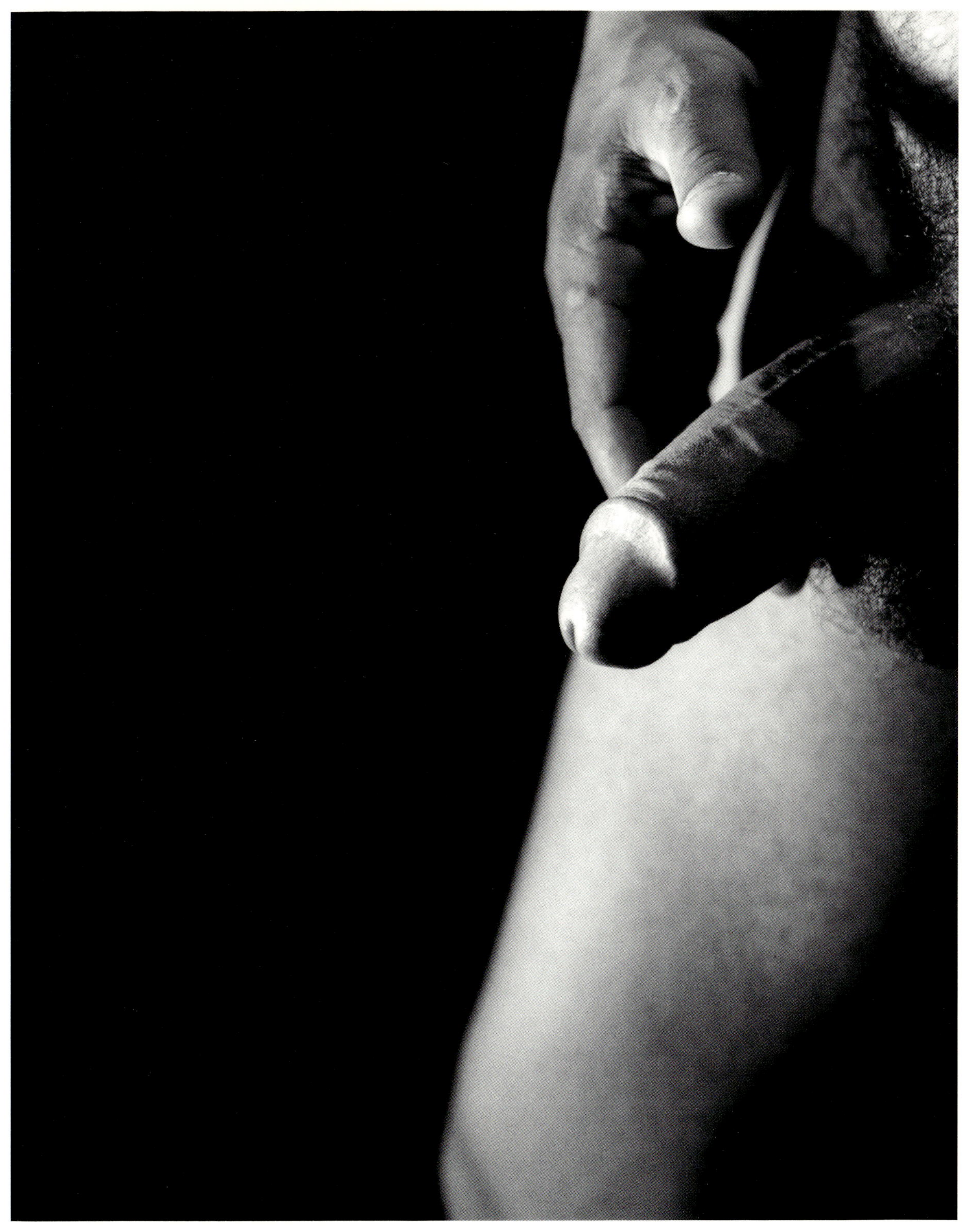

Senza Titolo, 1993

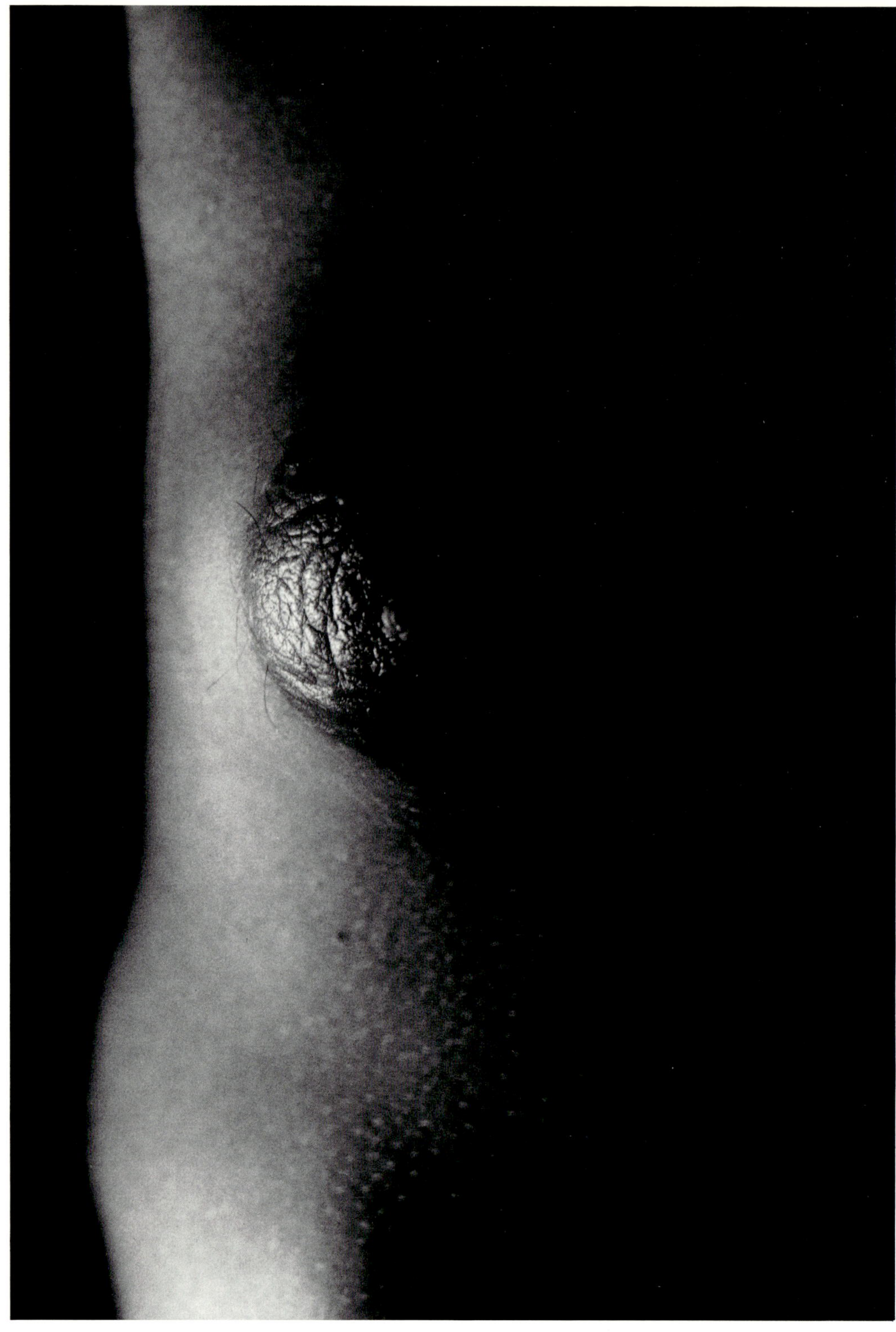

Emanuele, 1982

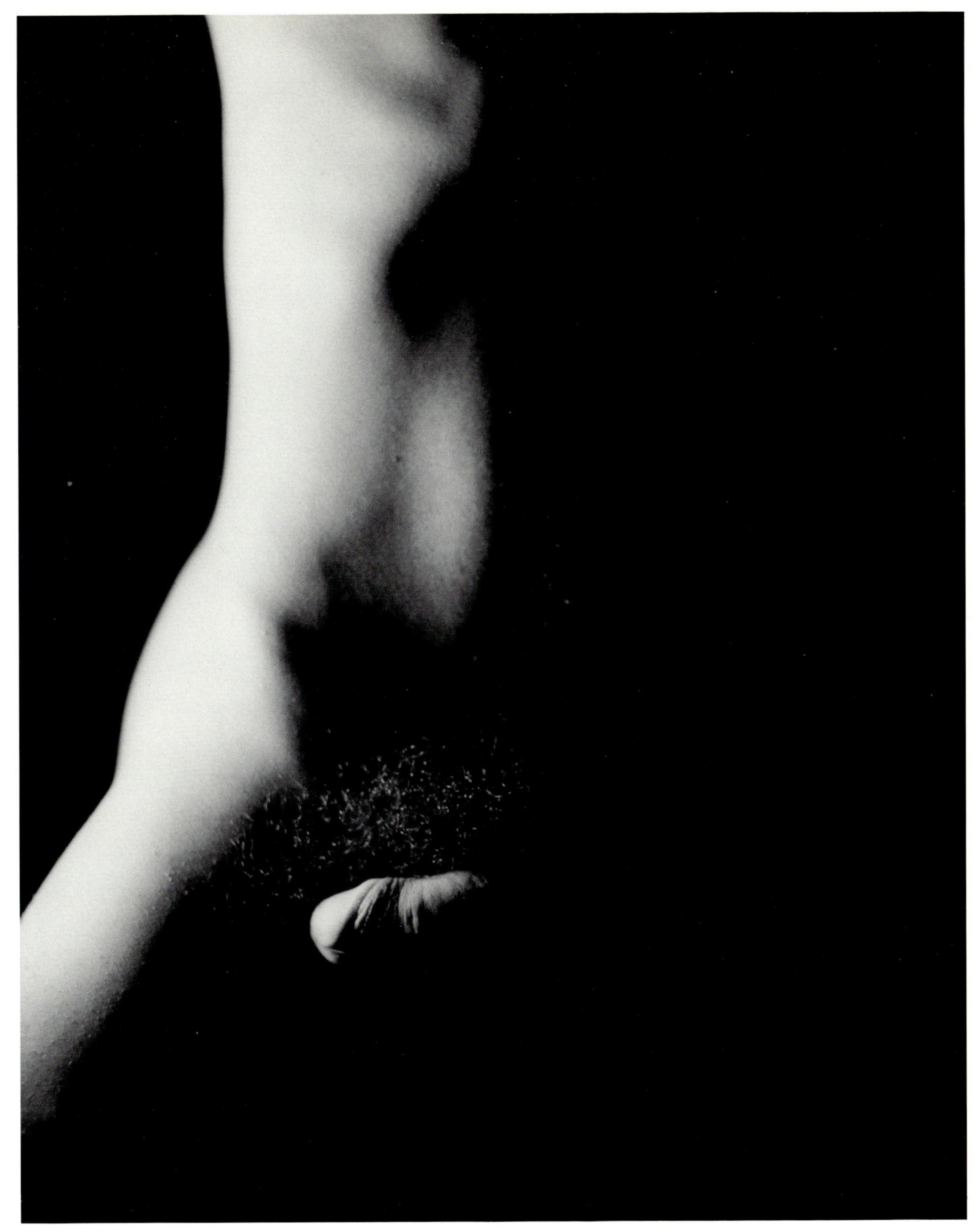

Teo, 1992

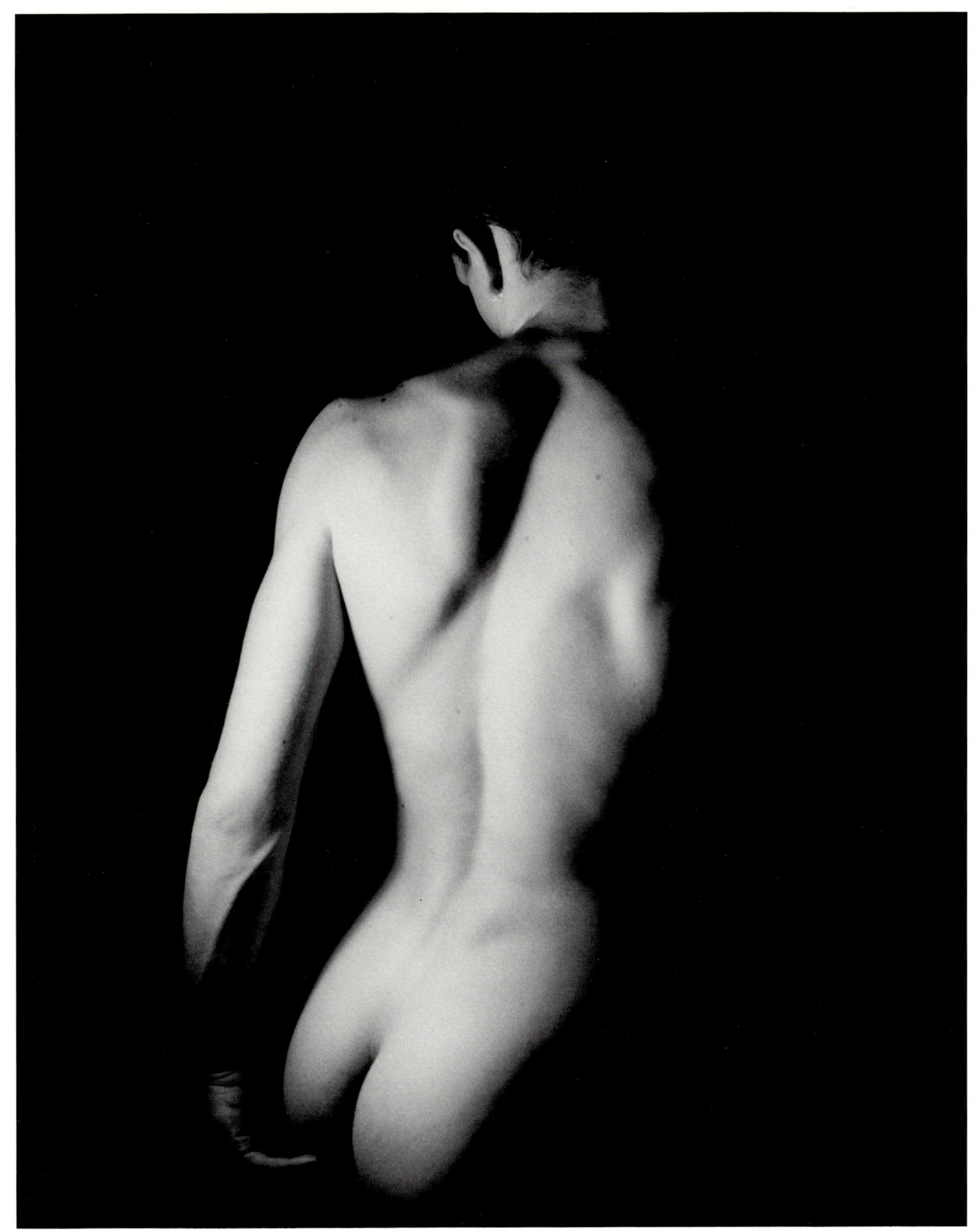

Dorso, 1990

Dino Pedriali: "Rappresentazione di Anima e di Corpo"

Maurizio Marini

The title paraphrase of a well-known early 17th-century musical composition offers, in my view, the key to an understanding of the work of Dino Pedriali. Figures such as time, death, the soul and the body are the undeniable (and hardly concealed) lyrical values of his expressive mode. Although communicated through the photographic medium, his language generates an abundance of sense impressions that go beyond the realm of the purely visual. Pedriali's youthful nudes tell a never-ending story, the story of eternal youth. It is a story whose protagonist is Man and his form, the term "form" in this case intended in its original Latin sense, meaning "beauty", namely the form of a being created in the image and likeness of God, who conceived and formed it in a warm, fatherly caress. A *deus artifex*, an artist (in keeping with the renaissance concept) for whom nature is art and the human being is both its measure and its ennoblement.

All of this is expressed in Dino Pedriali's work without mediating tones. The glorification of the created body is tantamount to the glorification of the creator; the one and the other are thus able to recognize and honor each other, unconstrained by the models and patterns of behavior prescribed by an aesthetic ethic which has no soul but is dominated by false shame (the very shame that is present in his vibrant portraits).

Nevertheless, the sense of evil (the negation of love) is the other – unavoidable –

aspect of these imaginative stories. Consequently, it is the shadow that confronts the light as an opaque, negative entity.

The bodies are thus permeated with an endogenous, thoroughly intellectual light that exists only to be set upon by shadows from without, both profound and mysterious. It is these that strive to consume the raw vitality until it withers away in the darkness of the senses.

On a figurative level, Dino Pedriali's message thus articulates itself in the perennial contest between light and shadow, which generate and extinguish each other in alternation in order to emphasize the coexistence of good and evil, of the spoken and the unspoken word, which finds its implicit parallel (and indeed its confirmation) in the tragic 16th-century painting of Caravaggio.

Pedriali does not, however, intend to revive Caravaggio in photography, nor does he mean to step beyond the limits of the image by means of a clever use of *chiaroscuro.* His originality pushes him to make use of light, as an inexhaustible means of discovering the emotions associated with the most hidden elements of universal being. One might also say that this is an artistic language that follows the path of a kind of anthropomorphic empiricism in which both the positive and the negative gain new values. These origins are reflected in the etymology of the word "photo-graph" itself, meaning "sign of light". And that is the existential credo of Dino Pedriali's camera eye.

Chronology

Dino Pedriali
Born in Rome in 1950;
lives and works in Rome

Solo exhibitions

1976 Galleria Romani Adami, Rome
Galleria Barozzi, Venice
1978 Galleria Inga Pin, Milan
Il Diagramma, Milan
1980 Galleria Il Fotogramma, Rome
1981 Museo Civico, Palazzo dei Diamanti, Ferrara
Galleria Ugo Ferranti, Rome
1982 Galleria Marginalia, Turin
Galleria Pan, Rome
Ikona Photo Gallery, Venice
Palazzo Corvaja, Taormina
1983 Galleria Il Ponte, Rome
Frankfurter Kunstverein, Frankfurt am Main
Centro Culturale San Fedele, Milan
Forum Stadtpark, Graz
Galleria Il Modulo, Terni
1984 Galleria Il Ponte, Rome
1985 Margaret Gallery, Taormina
1986 Frankfurter Kunstverein, Frankfurt am Main
Kunsthalle, Basel
Centro Culturale P.P. Pasolini, Agrigento
1987 "Silenzioso Abbraccio", Galleria La Bezuga, Florence
"Il Triangolo Rosa", Turin
"La Cacciata", Centro di Cultura Ausoni, Rome
"Omaggio ad Andy Warhol", Galleria Taget, Turin
1988 "Dino Pedriali", Pinacoteca Comunale di Ravenna (Santa Maria delle Croci), Ravenna
"Pier Paolo Pasolini: Testamento del Corpo" (anthology on P.P. Pasolini), Schauspielhaus, Düsseldorf; Berlin
1989 "L'Annunciazione", Galleria Il Ponte, Rome
"Testamento del corpo", Museum Arnhem (Netherlands)
1993 "Camera Oscura", Apeiron F.F. Club, Rome
"Dark Room", Teatro Colosseo, Rome
Arte Roma 1993, Galleria Il Ponte, Rome

Group exhibitions

1977 Galleria Lastaria, Rome
1978 "La Mano", Galleria dei Bibliofili, Milan
1981 "Fotografia e Teatro: Una busca parallela", Istituto Italiano di Cultura, Brazilia
"Taormina Fin de Siècle", Biblioteca Comunale, Taormina
Presenza nella Trasmissione Televisiva: "TG 2 Spazio Aperto/Foto", "Morire a Milano, Cronaca di un omicidio", "Man Ray": "Un Provocatore", "Memoria di un uomo scandoloso: P. P. Pasolini"; "Rudolf Nurejev", "Ritratti di Ragazzi"
"Fotografia e Teatro – Immagini della Ricerca Teatrale", Studio Carrieri, Martina Franca

1982 "Avanguardia/Transavanguardia", Spazio Giovani, Mura Aureliane, Rome
"Avventura: l'incisione", Chiesa di Palazzo Begni, Republic of San Marino
1983 "Critica ad Arte: Panorama della postcritica", Palazzo Lanfranchi, Pisa
"Body Beautiful?", Galleria Studio La Città, Verona
"Nuove Immagini Italiane", Galleria Il Ponte, Rome
1984 "Nuove Immagini Italiane/The Italian New Image", Staten Island Museum, New York
"Foto '84", Stichting Amsterdam Foto, Amsterdam
1985 "Das Aktfoto", Münchner Stadtmuseum, Munich; Frankfurter Kunstverein, Frankfurt am Main
"Selfportrait", Musée Cantonal des Beaux Arts, Lausanne
1986 "Oggetto Uomo", Castello Monumentale, Portovenere
"Männer sehen Männer", Galerie Hanns Christian Hoschek, Graz
1987 "Männer sehen Männer", Forum Böttcherstrasse, Bremen
"Neoclassicismo: Goethe in Italia", Centro di Cultura Ausoni, Rome
"Ignoto a me stesso", Mole Antonelliana, Turin
"Fotografia '87", Biennale Internazionale, Turin
"Nuove Acquisizioni", Pinacoteca Comunale di Ravenna (Santa Maria delle Croci)
"Il Nudo Maschile nella Fotografia del XIX e XX Secolo", Pinacoteca Comunale di Ravenna
1988 "Nuove Acquisizioni", Pinacoteca Comunale di Ravenna
"Dannunziana", Università Gabriele D'Annunzio, Pescara
1989 Il Ponte/Chicago International Art Exposition Chicago
Il Ponte Arte Fiera di Bologna
Ugo Ferranti/Kunstmesse, Basel
Ugo Ferranti/Kunstmesse Köln, Cologne
1990 Il Ponte/Arte Fiera di Bologna
Il Ponte/Chicago International Art Exposition
Arte Fiera Stoccolma/Galeria Ugo Ferranti
1993 Le Mente, L'immagine, Rome
1994 Attualissima, Progetto Firenze/Galleria Il Ponte
Art Chicago '94/Galleria Il Ponte

Bibliography

Agnese, M.L. "Pasolini era d'accordo?". Panorama. Milan, 14 March 1978.
Scimè, G. "Dino Pedriali". Fotozoom. Cittá del Messico, May 1978.
Gardin, Piero Berengo. Piero Berengo Gardin e Dino Pedriali in parallelo. Palazzo dei Diamanti, Ferrara, January 1981.
Mussa, I. "La Ricerca di Pedriali procede di volta in volta per scatti improvvisi". L'Avanti!, Rome, 29 March 1981.
Morelli, V. "Fotografia/Dino Pedriali". Corriere della Sera. Rome, 26 March 1981

Gardin, Piero Berengo. "Un fotografo che rifiuta il realismo". Paese Sera. Rome, 7 June 1981.

Semerano, G. "Inquadrature Ravvicinate". Il Tempo. Rome, 10 June 1981.

Carluccio, L. "Dino Pedriali, il corpo umano". Panorama. Milan, 29 June 1981.

Berettoni, L. La Luce come ragione d'essere. Galleria Pan, Rome, May 1982.

Vincitorio, F. "Fotografia". L' Espresso. Rome, 23 May 1982.

Micacchi, D. "Un fotogramma di luce per i volti tragici di giovani 'pasoliniani'". L'Unità. Rome, 11 June 1982

Falzone del Barbarò, M. "Pedriali mette a nudo il nudo". Il Giornale Nuovo. Milan, 15 July1982.

Alfonso, R. "Dino Pedriali". Segno. Pescara, May–June 1982.

Scimè, G. "Il Corpo come simbolo". Zoom. Milan, January 1983.

Siciliano, E. "Visi Nudi". Nuovi Argomenti. Milan, December 1982.

Gardin, Piero Berengo. "Questo fotografo lavora sul corpo". Paese Sera. Rome, 13 January 1983.

Pedriali, Dino and Alberto Moravia. Nove domande di Dino Pedriali ad Alberto Moravia. Ikona Photo Gallery, Venice, November 1982.

Calvenzi, G. "Dino Pedriali: Immagini di borgata". Il Fotografo. Milan, March 1983.

Berlinguer, B. "Pedriali Fotografo 'Guardone'". Il Messaggero. Rome, 17 March 1983.

Pigazzini, V. "Giovinezza irruente di borgata". Arte Bolaffi. Milan, May 1983.

Turroni, G. "Moravia, 'by Pedriali'". Corriere della Sera. Milan, 8 May 1983.

Gargiulo, G. "Un occhio magico". Il Mattino. Naples, 2 June 1983.

Mormorio, D. "Ti voglio fotografare nudo". Il Manifesto. Rome, 9 June 1983.

Mussa, I. "Dino Pedriali". Preface to Nuove Immagini Italiane. Il Ponte Editrice D'Arte, Rome, October 1983.

Griffi, G. Patroni. Galleria Il Modulo. Terni, November 1983.

Weiermair, P. "Ragazzi di vita". Wolkenkratzer, Frankfurt am Main, February/March 1984.

Scimè, G. "Il volto o il corpo nudi?". Progresso fotografico. Milan, July/August 1984.

Pedriali, D. "Nurejev: un mito denudato". Nuovi Argomenti. Editioni A. Mondadori No. 10, Vol. 3, Milan, April–June 1984.

Weiermair, P. "Dino Pedriali". Frankfurter Kunstverein, March 1984.

Mormorio, D. "Il nudo delle Aquile". Il Messaggero. Rome, 31 May 1985

Ammann, J.C. "Für Dino Pedriali". Frankfurter Kunstverein, March 1986.

Berettoni, L. "Dino Pedriali". Frankfurter Kunstverein, March 1986.

Scimè, G. Centro Culturale Editoriale P.P. Pasolini. Agrigento, October 1986.

Pedriali, D. "Seconda settimana d'ottobre 1975". Centro Culturale Editoriale P.P. Pasolini. Agrigento, October 1986.

Weiermair, P. (ed.). Männer sehen Männer. Verlag Photographie AG. Schaffhausen (CH), October 1986.

Mormorio, D. "Pasolini a nudo". Giornale di Sicilia. Catania, 14 November 1986.

Pedriali, D., Teobaldelli. "Intervista a Dino Pedriali". Babilonia, Milan, May 1987.

Mussa, I. "Dino Pedriali: La Cacciata". Editore Roma De Luca. Centro Cultura Ausoni, 1987.

Bandini, P. Nuove Acquisizioni. Pinacoteca Comunale di Ravenna, 1988.

Weiermair, P. Nuove Acquisizioni Pinacoteca Comunale di Ravenna, 1988.

Casorati, Cecilia. Dannunziana. Università Gabriele D'Annunzio, Pescara. Gruppo Editoriale Fabbri, Milan, July 1988.

Oliva, A. Bonito. "L'Essere dipende dall'apparire". Dannunziana. Gruppo Editoriale Fabbri, Milan, 1988.

Citati, P. "Narciso notturno in cerca di un io". Dannunziana. Gruppo Editoriale Fabbri, Milan, 1988.

Fernandez-Recatala, D. "La mort parfumée". Dannunziana. Gruppo Editoriale Fabbri, Milan, 1988.

Gareffi, A. "Fratte Gabri de Coty". Dannunziana. Gruppo Editoriale Fabbri, Milan, 1988.

Mussapi, R. "D'Annunzio e il Puer". Dannunziana. Gruppo Editoriale Fabbri, Milan, 1988.

Brizzi, A. Romani. "Dannunziana". Contemporanea International, Ed Il Quadrante. Turin, September/October 1988.

Battarra, E. "Dannunziana". Segno, No. 78. Pescara, October 1988.

Weiermair, P. Dino Pedriali in S. Maria delle Croci. Editione Essegi, Ravenna, 1988. Artefiera Bologna, 1989. Faenza Editrice S.p.A. Faenza, 1989.

Pedriali, D. "Tweede week van Oktober 1975". Pier Paolo Pasolini "Testamento del Corpo". Arturist, Arnhem, 1989.

Balmas, P. "Un'Annunciazione Nuda per Dino Pedriali". Il Piacere dell'Occhio. Trovaroma, La Repubblica. 29 April 1989.

Tentella, Z. "Rarità in bianco e nero". Il Tempo. 5 May 1989.

Gigliotti, G. "Corpi di luce che accendono la notte". Cultura, Paese Sera. 17 May 1989.

Treveri, Daniela. "La Verità in Camera Oscura". Il Tempo. 16 February 1993.

De Candia, Mario. "Una geografia dell'uomo creata con l'obiettivo". Trovaroma, 25 February 1993.

De Candia, Mario. "Dark Room". Trovaroma. 17 June 1993.

Garrone, Nico. "Obiettivo su Pier Paolo Pasolini" La Repubblica. 23 June 1993.

Illustrated publications

Man Ray. Edizioni Magma, Rome, 1975.

Pier Paolo Pasolini. Edizioni Magma, Rome, 1975.

Andy Warhol. Edizione Magma, Rome, 1976.

Catalogues

Galleria Inga Pin. Il Diagramma. Edizioni Raron Book, Milan, 1978.

Palazzo dei Diamanti (ed. Piero Berengo Gardin). Ferrara, 1981.

Taormina Fin de Siècle (ed. Italo Mussa). Biblioteca Comunale, Taormina, 1981.

Galleria Pan (ed. Luigi Berettoni). Rome, 1982.

Ikona Photo Gallery. Venice, 1982.

Critica ad Arte: Panorama della post-critica (ed. Achille Bonito Oliva). Palazzo Lanfranchi, Pisa, 1983.

Dino Pedriali (ed. Peter Weiermair). Frankfurter Kunstverein, Frankfurt am Main, 1986.

Dino Pedriali (ed. Peter Weiermair). Kunsthalle, Basel, 1986.

Omaggio a Pier Paolo Pasolini (ed. Giuliana Scimè). Centro Culturale Editoriale Pier Paolo Pasolini, Agrigento, 1986.

Silenzioso Abbraccio (ed. Italo Mussa). Galleria La Bezuga, Florence, 1987.

La Cacciata (ed. Italo Mussa). Centro di Cultura Ausoni, Rome, 1987.

Books

Il mestiere di fotografo (ed. Diego Mormorio and Mario Verdone). Edizioni Romana Libri Alfabeto, Rome, April 1985.

Männer sehen Männer (ed. Peter Weiermair). Verlag Photographie AG, Schaffhausen (CH), 1986.

Das verborgene Bild (ed. Peter Weiermair). Ariadne Verlag, Vienna, 1987.

Periodicals

Nuovi Argomenti, No. 1, Vol. 3. Edizioni A. Mondadori. Milan, 1982.

Nuovi Argomenti, No. 4, Vol. 3. Edizioni A. Mondadori. Milan, 1982

Il Fotografo. Edizioni A. Mondadori. Milan, March 1983.

Espressione, No. 1. Edizioni Il Fotogramma. Rome, January–March 1980.

Grandi Temi della Fotografia – La Foto Sociale, part 3. Fratelli Fabbri Editori. Milan, 1983.

Progresso Fotografico. Milan, July/August 1984.

Wolkenkratzer. Frankfurter Kunstverein. February/March 1984.

Nuovi Argomenti, No. 10, Vol. 3. Edizioni A. Mondadori. Milan, 1984.

Vanity. Edizioni Condé Nast. Milan, July 1984.

Nuovi Argomenti, No. 20, Vol. 3. Edizioni A. Mondadori. Milan, 1986.

Portfolios:

Nuove Immagini Italiane: Cinque Pittori e un Fotografo (ed. Italo Mussa). Edizioni Il Ponte Editrice d'Arte. Rome, 1982.

Avventura – L'Incisione (ed. Italo Mussa). Edizioni La Virgola. Rome, 1982.

List of plates

13 Portrait of a youth, 1981, 12x16 in.
14 Portrait of a youth, 1978, 12x16 in.
15 Al Buco, 1976, 12x16 in.
16 Al Buco, 1976, 12x16 in.
17 Al Buco, 1976, 12x16 in.
19 Tonino dei Ponti, 1982, 16x20 in.
20 Portrait of a youth, 1981, 12x16 in.
21 Portrait of a youth, 1977, 12x16 in.
22 Claudio, 1980, 12x16 in.
23 Claudio, 1980, 12x16 in.
24 Claudio, 1980, 12x16 in.
25 Claudio, 1980, 12x16 in.
26 Claudio, 1980, 12x16 in.
27 Claudio, 1980, 12x16 in.
28 Untitled, 1981, 12x16 in.
29 Untitled, 1981, 12x16 in.
30 Claudio, 1980, 12x16 in.
31 Untitled, 1981, 12x16 in.
33 The Brothers Romolo and Claudio, 1984, 16x20 in.
34 Carmine, 1984, 16x20 in.
35 Filippo and Antonio, 1983, 16x20 in.
36 Untitled, 1981, 12x16 in.
37 Marcello, 1984, 16x20 in.
38 My study of a nude, 1984, 16x20 in.
39 Friends from the area, 1984, 16x20 in.
40 Pasqualino, 1983, 16x20 in.
41 Friends from the area, 1984, 16x20 in.
42 The Brothers Romolo and Claudio, 1984, 16x20 in.
43 Bruno, 1984, 16x20 in.
44 Ali, 1982, 16x20 in.
45 Albino, 1982, 16x20 in.
46 Bruno, 1984, 16x20 in.
47 Carmine, 1984, 16x20 in.

48 Nuccio, 1984, 16x20 in.
49 Nuccio, 1984, 16x20 in.
50 Nuccio, 1984, 16x20 in.
51 Filippo and Antonio, 1983, 16x20 in.
53 Fabio, 1985, 16x20 in.
54 Gennaro, 1984, 16x20 in.
55 Edoardo, 1984, 16x20 in.
56 Carmine, 1984, 16x20 in.
57 Franchino, 1985, 16x20 in.
58 Michele, 1985, 16x20 in.
59 Andrea, 1985, 16x20 in.
60 Gianni, 1985, 16x20 in.
61 Sandro, 1985, 16x20 in.
62 Ian, 1984, 16x20 in.
63 Gennaro, 1984, 16x20 in.
64 Ian, 1984, 16x20 in.
65 The Gipsy (Homage to Pier Paolo Pasolini), 1984, 16x20 in.
67 Roberto, 1985, 16x20 in.
68 Davide, 1985, 16x20 in.
69 Gennaro, 1984, 16x20 in.
70 Gennaro, 1984, 16x20 in.
71 Umberto, 1983, 16x20 in.
73 David and Goliath, 1985, 16x20 in.
74 Gianni, 1985, 16x20 in.
75 Roberto, 1985, 16x20 in.
77 Edoardo, 1984, 16x20 in.
78 Arturo, 1985, 16x20 in.
79 The Brothers Romolo and Claudio, 1984, 16x20 in.
81 Pino, 1987, 12x16 in.
83 Rudolf Nureyev, 1984, 12x16 in.
84 Ivo, 1987, 12x16 in.
85 Torsion, 1989, 12x16 in.
87 Augusto, 1989, 12x16 in.
88 Homage to Werther 2, 1989, 12x16 in.
89 Homage to Werther 1, 1987, 12x16 in.
91 Imaginary selfportrait, 1989, 12x16 in.
92 Ettore, 1989, 12x16 in.
93 Fertility, 1989, 12x16 in.
95 Claudio, 1987, 12x16 in.
96 Mercurio, 1993, 12x16 in.
97 Boy from Trani, 1989, 12x16 in.
99 Metamorphosis, 1990, 12x16 in.
100 Oliviero, 1992, 12x16 in.
101 Youth from S. Paolo di Civitate, 1991, 12x16 in.
103 Untitled, 1993, 12x16 in.
104 Emanuele, 1982, 16x20 in.
105 Teo, 1992, 12x16 in.
107 Back, 1990, 12x16 in.

Translation by John S. Southard

Prints made by Franco Bugionovi

Typography and layout by Grafikdesign Peter Wassermann, Andrea Hostettler, Fluringen, Switzerland

Photolithography by Paul Robert Wilk, Seulberg, Germany, and Repro Fuchs GmbH, Salzburg, Austria

Printed and bound by Passavia Druckerei GmbH, Passau, Germany

ISBN 3-905514-38-9